MW00951806

Rilke's Art of Metric Melody

VOLUME ONE

Note on the Frontispiece

My friend Shahid Alam's calligraphic art work, reproduced with his kind permission, offers the last 6 lines of Rilke's "Liebes-Lied" or "Love Song," poem 3 in this book, written in alternating lines of Arabic and German. Here is the German:

> Doch alles, was uns anrührt, dich und mich,
> nimmt uns zusammen wie ein Bogenstrich,
> der aus zwei Saiten *eine* Stimme zieht.
> Auf welches Instrument sind wir gespannt?
> Und welcher Geiger hat uns in der Hand?
> O süßes Lied.

In English:

> But everything that touches you and me
> Takes us together, unifyingly,
> Two notes, one tone, in single bow-stroke fleet.
> Upon what instrument our stringing? and
> Of whom the holding violinist-hand?
> O song, O sweet.

Writing the excerpt interlinearly brings together, as the two violin pitches combine in the doublestop or two-note chord played by the bowstroke, two entities harmoniously in one: Arabic and German, east and west. So Rilke unites two cultures by composing a wonderful sonnet in western lyrical tradition about "Muhammad's Calling" (see dialogue 172). And in an unpublished wisdom lyric perhaps originally intended for *West-East Divan* (given as poem 242 in Bidney's dialogic translation of 2010), Johann Wolfgang von Goethe writes:

> Who knows himself and others well
> No longer may ignore:
> Occident and Orient dwell
> Separately no more.
>
> 'Twixt two worlds I love the way
> Back and forth a man can sway;
> So between the East and West
> Moving to and fro's the best.

كل ما يمسُّنا أنتَ و أنا

Doch alles, was uns anrührt, dich und mich,

كالقوس يضمُّنا

nimmt uns zusammen wie ein Bogenstrich,

يسحب نغمًا بوترين

der aus zwei Saiten eine Stimme zieht.

على أي آله شُدِّنا؟

Auf welches Instrument sind wir gespannt?

بأنامل أيّ عارف حزنا؟

Und welcher Geiger hat uns in der Hand?

أيا غنيّة عذبة!

süßes Lied

Rilke

Rilke's Art of Metric Melody

Form-Faithful Translations
with Dialogic Verse Replies

VOLUME ONE:
NEW POEMS I AND II

MARTIN BIDNEY

Dialogic
Poetry
Press

Copyright © 2017 by Martin Bidney
Dialogic Poetry Press
Vestal, New York

All Rights Reserved

ISBN 13: 978-1976596421
ISBN 10: 1976596424

Printed in the United States of America

Available from Amazon at
http://www.amazon.com/dp/1976596424

The translator/author wishes to
dedicate this book
to his dear friend and mentor,
the artist and calligrapher

Shahid Alam

Contents

Introduction: Empathy in Melodic and Metrical Art

This book portrays the many-sided empathy that awakens when we write, read, respond to, and/or translate a poem. The varied empathies arising here are of several interacting kinds. A number are embodied in the poetic experiences of Rainer Maria Rilke (1875–1926), my favorite modern poet and likely, I think, one of the finest who ever lived. Other empathies come across in my own daily activity and way of life as I try to be Rilke's form-faithful translator and effective conversation partner in verse. The Bohemian-Austrian poet and I are engaged in mutually complementary empathies throughout our shared project.

The Greek-derived word "empathy," like the German synonym "Einfühlung," means "feeling-in" or "feeling into." In her recent book *You Must Change Your Life: The Story of Rainer Maria Rilke and Auguste Rodin* (Norton 2016), art critic Rachel Corbett shows that Rilke's term "Einsehen" ("seeing-in" or "seeing into") is the poet's word for his own, highly personal kind of empathetic writing (*C* 99), something learned with the help of his devoted discipleship to the sculptor Auguste Rodin. American poetry lovers will think immediately of Gerard Manley Hopkins' word "inscape" for the same mode of feeling and approach as in Rilkean "inseeing."

I

Let me invite you into the workshop where my Rilkean and Rilke-responsive lyrics are crafted, to sample how empathies arise. The word "lyric" means "singable to a lyre." Rilke and I are faithful to the ancient Greek tradition that equated poetry and music, so that prizes were awarded at the Olympics to melodious poets as to athletes. Every one of our poems is meant to be read aloud.

Why not start, then, with an unfolding of the empathy that can rise when we first read a Rilke poem aloud—the empathy that's rooted in the bliss of pronouncing, singing, and feeling something in the German language? Here is Rilke's panther poem, one of his best-loved word songs, often appearing in anthologies. I'll take it as my representative sample of the first book of lyrics I translate in this volume, Rilke's *Neue Gedichte* or what I'm calling *New Poems I* (1907). Even if you don't read German you can still begin to savor the verse, as I'll show in a moment. (The two poems I transcribe in this Introduction are from Rainer Maria Rilke: *Neue Gedichte / Der neuen Gedichte anderer Teil*, Berliner Ausgabe, 2016, 4th edition, ed. Michael Holzinger.)

Der Panther
Im Jardin des Plantes, Paris

Sein Blick ist von Vorübergehn der Stäbe
so müd geworden, daß er nichts mehr hält.
Ihm ist, als ob es tausend Stäbe gäbe
und hinter tausend Stäben keine Welt.

Der weiche Gang geschmeidig starker Schritte,
der sich im allerkleinsten Kreise dreht,
ist wie ein Tanz von Kraft um eine Mitte
in der betäubt ein Großer Wille steht.

Nur manchmal schiebt der Vorhang der Pupille
sich lautlos auf —. Dann geht ein Bild hinein,
geht durch der Glieder angespannte Stille—
und hört in Herzen auf zu sein.

It's wonderful to hear these lines read aloud on the net, but
even without doing that, you can get a musical thrill from
all the new sounds if you just practice making them. [Note
that "ß" is just a way of writing "ss."] "U" will be like "oo" as
in "through"; "eh" will sound like our English word "eh?";
"o" is reasonably close to the sound in English "or"; "ie" will
be like our "ee," and "ei" as in "eye" or "high." Ordinarily an
"a" has the "ah" sound as in "father." But with the two-dot
umlaut sign above the "a" we have an abbreviation of "ae."
So the "ä" gives the vowel a sound more like the "a" in the
English word "May." That's an easy adjustment to make. A
little trickier is the "ü" letter, which is an abbreviation of
"ue," a hybrid of "oo" and "ee." To make this sound, put your
mouth in the position to say "oo," then adjust your tongue
as if it wanted to say "ee." Now make a sound, and it will
be "ü." "Au" is like "Ow!" and "äu" is like "Oy!" "Der" pretty
much rhymes with "dare," and "hört" sounds pretty much
like "hurt." The "e" at the end of a word is pronounced as
in "egg," though a bit more lightly. "St" is pronounced "sht,"
"sp" like "shp." "Ch" in "durch" or "manchmal" or "weich"
(also the final "g" in "geschmeidig") is like a "sh" mixed with
the "y" of "yellow." (You shape a circle with your mouth to
focus the air; the sound you get will be that of a steaming
tea-kettle right before it whistles.) "Th" is "t" and "s" is "z"
and "z" is "ts."

Little children derive endless pleasure from learning to

make strange sounds, and if you retain anything of this childhood capacity for tone-imitating joy, you will see immediately how empathy is awakened not only for a particular poem but for an entire language. The empathy grows on account of the sensuous pleasure of making new and beautiful word sounds, added to the novelty of the brain activity involved. Language learning is at least as fine a re-creative recreation as fishing, cooking, hunting, sewing, hiking, swimming ...

It isn't true that a rose by any other name would smell as sweet. The sounds made to express a picture or concept or emotion give these experiences a distinct sensuous and intellectual "feel." Because of the diversely musical nature of verbal sounds, to speak a new language isn't just like playing a new musical instrument, it's more like playing a new *orchestra* of instruments! What an astonishingly diversified skill! To read a poem in the poet's own language is to practice an empathetic "inhearing" into the complex of mental and physical actions that are the sonorous, or canorous (singing), mellifluent body of the author's expression. As you get more practice in using your new language with native speakers, you'll notice that none of the vowels, none of the consonants, is *exactly* like its approximate counterpart in English. The "orchestra" really is filled with somewhat different instruments—and in hearing these fascinating little differences you can become an ever-better performing musician in reciting. Every time I go to Germany I pick up new clues about precise refinements in pronunciation. On May 17, 2017 I gave a lecture in German ("Juden und Christen im Koran," or "Jews and Christians in the Qur'an") at the St. Thomas Lutheran Church in Berlin to help celebrate the 500th anniversary of the Protestant Reformation as part of their series of commemorative events on interreligious dialogue called "Einandersehen"—"Seeing One Another." You acquire an excitingly new and beautiful identity when you offer a presentation in a wonderful, welcoming setting and in such a dramatic, lovely, and colorful language. "Einandersehen" can be interpreted as "Mutual Empathy."

The empathy one feels for a new language is particularly intense in "lyric" verse, which, as I've indicated, has been felt since the Greeks to be a kind of music, a type of singing. Lyric verse is musical because it contains harmonies, rhythms, and a melodic flow uniting the functions of these. Ordinary conversational speech (prose) has similar features, but they are foregrounded, intensified, concentrated in verse. That's why verse is traditionally called "singing," as when Homer begins his *Odyssey* by entreating, "Sing in me, Muse, and tell, through me, the story ... ." He's asking the goddess of poetry to sing through him: she will speak within, and he will utter (a word that really means "outer") what she internally gives him. Vergil says at the start of the *Aeneid*, "Arms and the man I sing ... ." Greek and Roman poets called themselves singers, and with good reason. They wrote and performed word songs.

What is a verbal "harmony"? It's the recurrence of a vowel or consonant with one exactly like it or closely resembling it. I've noticed that our finest lyrical minds attempt, whether consciously or intuitively by instinct, to ensure that if a given consonant or vowel is used in a lyrical poem, the same or a closely related one will appear also, turning what would have been an anomaly into a harmony. Shakespeare observed this rule rigorously in his book of sonnets. Look at the vowel harmonies in our German "Panther": the opening stanza is abundant in the sound "ä." The first two lines add the harmony of a double "ü." As stanza two opens we have the harmony of the quadruple "ei" in the first two lines, then the double "a" in line 3 (plus another "a" as the first half of the double vowel "ei" in "eine") and two paired similar sounds "äu" and "o" in line 4. The repeated "a" of line 3 harmonizes with a triple "a" in the first line of stanza three, and in the second line of that stanza the "au" and "ei" sounds each contain an "ah" as the first half of the two-part vowel sound. I could do the same analytic treatment with consonants, but I think the idea is perhaps clear enough.

Harmonious vowels and consonants charm the ear, but to feel really singable—to become "word songs"—they need meter, regular rhythm, too. What, then, is rhythm in German or English verse? It's a pattern of beats maintained by alternations between "strong" or heavier and "weak" or lighter syllables. Look at the first line of the second stanza: "der WEI-che GANG ge-SCHMEI-dig STAR-ker SCHRIT-te." You can count the syllables like this: "and ONE, and TWO, and THREE, and FOUR, and FIVE, and." Five real rhythmic beats. Try the next line: "der SICH, im AL,-ler-KLEIN,-sten KREI,-se DREHT." This time we hear "and ONE, and TWO, and THREE, and FOUR, and FIVE." All the lines of the poem have this five-beat rhythm except the last: "und HÖRT, im HER,-zen AUF, zu SEIN"—and ONE, and TWO, and THREE, and FOUR"—likely shortened to show the dying away of the world in the panther's heart: he can't make it through all the five beats of his final line. Never was the taking away of a single beat more deeply moving in a verse.

We have independent testimony regarding Rilke's feeling for the rhythmic power of words. Writer Stefan Zweig tells that "walking with Rilke in Paris" was always a treat because it meant "seeing the importance of the most insignificant things, as if with new eyes; he noticed every little thing, and if the names on the brass plates of businesses seemed to him rhythmical he would recite them out loud" (*Only Yesterday,* University of Nebraska Press, 2009, 167). New eyes and new ears. I'm a bit like that: seeing in a German parking lot that cars parked illegally would be "towed away at the owner's expense," I noted how rhythmical were the words "kostenpflichtig abgeschleppt" (ONE and, TWO and, THREE and, FOUR—four trochees with a missing syllable in the final one—that is, "trochaic tetrameter catalectic").

The feeling of melody awakes when you hear how the harmonious recurrings of vowels and of consonants combine with the recurring rhythms of the steady lines. Each two-syllable unit ("and ONE" or "and TWO") is called a foot, or rhythm structure unit, and the foot that has the structure "weak STRONG" is called an iamb. Rilke's typical line in his panther poem is five iambs or iambic feet (with or without an extra syllable at the end), the same rhythm as Shakespeare mainly employs throughout his plays and in most of his 154 sonnets. All kinds of subtleties arise, as you'll feel when you "sing" or read aloud. Not all the "heavy" syllables are equally heavy, not all the "light" ones equally light. In the second line of my sample above, the "SICH" isn't nearly so strongly emphasized as the next heavy syllable, AL-. Because the often tiny differences in weight can't be registered simply with capitals and lower case, to some degree my sample lines are (over)simplified. But simplified organizational patterns are needed as mental ways of orienting a person to a basic structure whose variations then come to be savored more and more with increasing confidence and experience in reading aloud (whether physically or to the mental ear, the inner ear of the imaginer-actor-reciter).

If English vowels and consonants aren't the same as German ones, the vowel and consonant harmonies in an English translation can't be the same as those in the German original. And if we think (as I do) that a rose by another name will smell rather different, then even the feelings and concepts conveyed in the English won't be quite the same as those conveyed in the German. So a question may arise. Will what the English poem translator says ever be the same as what the German poem writer said?

To approach an answer, I suggest reformulating the question. If a lyrical poem is more a song than a speech, maybe we ought to ask not what is "said" but rather what is "sung." I often go to vocal concerts where a song's poem-text in a foreign language is translated into an English prose text which, though it may be printed in "lines" to make it look like a poem, shouldn't fool anybody. Why? Because in trying to show what the poet "said," the talky but unmusical prose text tends to destroy what the poet "sang." It lets me down, so I generally ignore it. Prose supertitles in opera, too, are likely to destroy the poetry in the foreign language text because they are often dull, flat, and inartistic. Well-translated librettos in verse, by contrast, may delight the ear.

Asking a new question, then, can a poet translate what another poet *sang*? If we put the matter this way, then we are more reasonably comparing *two works of art*. If two languages are like two sets of different instruments, isn't a translation rather like a transcription or rewriting of a musical piece for a different instrumental ensemble? It isn't exactly the same composition, but the art works are effectively *analogous*.

Considering the structures of audible beauty in an original foreign-language lyric and in an English translation of it as *analogous* will help us think clearly about what verse translations are. Some people have doubted whether verse translation is possible at all. It isn't possible if we think of it in the narrow sense as a duplication of exactly the same beauties: obviously that can't be done if the resources of sound are different in German and in English. But once we hear a translation as the creation of a set of *analogous* beauties, translation into verse becomes not only a logical possibility but a thrilling challenge, and a thing of wonder when done well.

What then might help the translator create a poem convincingly analogous to the original? I would answer: *empathy* (or, if you like, inseeing, inhearing, inscape). Empathy is a subset of love: feeling-into is a feeling-with. First, you fall in love with the poem you're re-singing. You pay detailed attention to the vowel harmonies, consonant harmonies, rhythmic structures, and the melodic flow that sweeps all of these along in a process permitting the syntax to have subtle variations in tempo. Then you try to "transcribe" all this into analogous features of your own composition, re-scored for your own language, your own instrumental ensemble.

Did I carry out this program in my panther poem, translating that of Rilke? See what you think:

The Panther
in the Botanic Garden, Paris

His look has by the passing of the bars
Become so weary it can hold no more.
A seeming thousand of them, constant jars
To mind: behind them, there's no world in store.

The walk, so gentle-flexible and strong,
Small roundings making, daily littler still,
Is like a dance of power, overlong,
Around a mighty though a deafened will.

Eye-pupils' curtain will at times be viewed
In quiet raised—A picture suddenly
Will enter limbs' extended quietude
And in the heart will cease to be.

You can hear the close analogy of the iambic pentameter rhythms, including the last tetrameter line a foot shorter than the rest. The vowel harmonies are analogously abundant: has-passing, thousand-roundings, constant-walk-strong, gentle-flexible-deafened, littler-still, bars-jars-heart, world-curtain, pupils'-quietude, cease-be. Consonant harmonies include bars/behind, littler-still-like-will, pupils'-picture. The most important result of studying the vowel and consonant harmonies is to show that nearly everything harmonizes or "rhymes" with something else in the poem, so that rhymes at the end of lines are merely the most dramatic example of the constant thorough-rhyming that goes on within and among the lines. There's no way you can be a verse translator, achieving complexities like these, without being a poet yourself. Empathy for the writer you admire can only rise to an adequately creative level sufficient to do the work justice if you perfect the craftsmanlike skills enabling you to offer a thorough-going analogy to his or her treasured mode-and-meaning of composition, the way the poet's lyric spirit is *melodically embodied.*

Rachel Corbett's book, cited above, shows that empathy, the quality I find central to good translation, is itself the subject matter of many of the poems where Rilke embodies it. Empathy, she notes—or *Einfühlung,* a German word introduced during the poet's lifetime—was the subject of considerable philosophic theorizing by early 20th century thinkers, notably Theodor Lipps and Wilhelm Worringer. Corbett feels, however, that Rilke absorbed empathy in a more direct and practical way by observing the daily sculptural activity of Auguste Rodin when he was the latter's secretary. Rodin paid the minutest attention to every detail of the person he was sculpting, making models to embody various points of view, getting to know the cherished model from every perspective. But even while his penetrating gaze focused on the model, he often wouldn't look at the clay he was shaping. He would instead feel the growing life of the developing sculpture unfold, e-volve or turn outward, from within as his hands coaxed it forth. The form is not imitated so much as the coming-to-life of that form is emulated.

Corbett evokes the way Rodin's example shaped Rilke's feeling of *Einsehen* or inseeing:

> Inseeing ... took into account the object's point of view. It had as much to do with making things human as it did with making humans *thing.*
>
> If faced with a rock, for instance, one should stare deep

into the place where its rockiness begins to form. Then the observer should keep looking until his own center starts to sink with the stony weight of the rock forming inside him, too. It is a kind of perception that takes place within the body, and it requires the observer to be both the seer and the seen. To observe with empathy, one sees not only with the eyes but with the skin. (C 99)

If the rockiness of the rock has to be felt as it "begins to form" deep within a central place, in order that the "center" of the "inseer," as well, may begin to form an analogous outward-growing rockiness, the Rilkean inseer begins to sound like the Rodinesque be-holder, who coaxes forth the being in what he holds, making it be, cause it to come out or become. What Rilke and Rodin both want, I suggest, is a seeing outward from the center of self and object, the seeing-and-feeling of a becoming, of a process.

Rodin the sculptor and Rilke the poet don't imitate an inseen object with their clay or words, they emulate the life process of the object, its becoming.

It strikes me that while the thing-as-process unfolds in its own unique local space-time, *we feel* the unfolding of that space-time, as well. This may help account for the metaphysical or mystical aura to which many Rilke readers attest. I would call it an ontological dimension. Ontology is the study of reality and unreality, of being and nothingness; and in Rilke's poem, this is the central topic. Watching the panther's reality waste away in its local space-time, we feel, in its depth and our own, the way its vital being-and-becoming, its changeful reality in time, is unrelentingly eroded by the compulsory and fatal nothingness of the cage that seals it off from reality, from meaningful activity with other creatures. So, for all the highlighted thingliness of what Rilke called his "thing poems," the focus is never on substance or substantiality (suggesting an underlying solidity or a solid base) but on the process-life of the object in the space-time where it dwells.

We see that process-life so clearly in "The Panther"! We never get a look at the outside of the panther as a thing. Stanza one: he glances about and what he keeps on seeing wearies him, a Piranesi dungeon of endlessly multiplying cage or jail-bars. Stanza two: his will is deafened by the loud dance of power that is a mere masquerade, the pointless, debilitating sound of his endless hellish roundings of the cage that become like the ever more constricting circles of a narrowing cone in a Dantescan Hell. Stanza three: when he raises weary eyelids, an image enters him, only to die at his deadened center. Dare we go to the zoo after this? Empathy has made his imprisoned spirit into our own, for we are bound in the distorted space-time peculiar to his confinement. We go through a processual sequence with ontologic import. The unreality of caged being is felt within, unfolded from within, and it returns inward to a death. We are viewing the effects of the increasing awareness of the torment of unreality on the way a creature must live—and die—within its own space-time. The degree to which I've been able to convey this ontologic mindset with empathy in my translation is proportional to the degree of detailed attention I've empathetically paid to vowel and consonant harmonies, rhythms, melodic flow in the German text. Since the issues raised—about being and becoming, space and time, life and death—bring with them imaginative and emotional intensity, all musical resources need to be applied to convey so much implicit feeling.

II

To a startling degree, every Rilke lyric is like "The Panther" (or like "Archaic Torso of Apollo," the second exemplary poem I want to examine here)—a matter of being and becoming, dream and reality, space and time, life and death. Rilke is, in my experience, the foremost ontological poet. Because this dimension of his thought and feeling is at once so wide in implication and so intently focused on the concrete existence of a thing or creature as we watch it develop from within, Rilke will often approach the limit of what can be sung in language. The means of expression he employs to do this are so intricate and subtle that we must follow faithfully the windings of his syntax as well as the rhythm and harmony of his words. Together they provide the means whereby music can aid speech in winging the distance from heart-thought to expression.

Applying empathy, then, I tried to translate a poem that itself embodies the empathy the poet has learned and now can teach. Empathy, however, is not the same as discipleship: it goes farther and wider. I could imagine adding to Corbett's book title an extra subheading: *The Disciple Becomes a Dialogue Partner.* As secretary to Rodin, Rilke wrote down the latter's vigorous affirmations of aesthetic principle as if he were "a young Plato recording the words of Socrates" (C132). Not only did Rilke write an effusive monograph about Rodin; even the pages of *Letters to a Young Poet*—Rilke's book best known to Americans—are filled with reverberations of the Frenchman's oracular voice (Cviii). Later, though, the father-figure had to be transcended if the "prodigal son" (Rilke's favorite Bible personage) was to make his way into the territory of the lonely and unloved, where in the emptiness he could grow. Mentorship, never quite renounced, must yet yield space to rebellion, and Rilke writes to his wife Nietzschean-sounding maxims proclaiming himself no longer a pupil (C 209). Describing Rodin's sculptural creativity a moment ago I wrote: "The form is not imitated so much as the coming-to-life of that form is emulated." Rilke did not merely imitate (copy) Rodin, he emulated (rivaled) him.

My feeling as I translate into verse a poem written in German is that of an athlete engaged in friendly sportsmanlike rivalry. Given that my structure of harmonies, rhythms, and streams of melody won't be the same as the German one but rather analogous, there's no logical reason why it can't be, in its somewhat different way, not less beautiful than the original but equally beautiful. Or maybe even lovelier? Why not? To the clichéd and arbitrary formula "Translator = Traitor" I reply with the possibility that "Translator = Greater." Competition will widen the lungs of the runner and sweeten the tones of the singer. After I had translated "Hegira" for my dialogic book *West-East Divan— The Poems, with "Notes and Essays": Goethe's Intercultural Dialogues* (SUNY Press, 2010, 1–2)—I showed the lyric to a scholar-colleague, who said, "Goethe's poem is good-humored, and yours is even lighter." Does that mean it's any better? Unlikely, though not impossible. But the encouraging comment put me into such a good mood that it animated my verse "reply" using Goethe's own jaunty, bouncy four-beat stanza form, appropriate to his party-like symposium with his soul-brother Hafiz and his lady-friend Laila:

> Writing is an Eden-wine
> When in rhythm and in rhyme
> I felicitate a fest,
> Zithering your life with zest.
> Trochees lighten any load
> When we quickly hit the road.
>   (ll. 7–12, 294)

Rilke is my Rodin, and I seek not to imitate but to emulate him. The most innovative way I do this—with genuine empathy, I hope—is to offer, as I did with Goethe's *Divan*, a book of verse dialogues. To each rendering of a Rilke lyric in the present volume I add an additional poem as "reply," a conversational intervention, the grateful and eager response of a happy collocutor.

To Rilke's masterly poem "The Panther" my reply has two parts. First I translate a sonnet by Russian Symbolist

poet Konstantin Balmont (1867–1942) called "The Panther."
(Note: all translations in this book are my own unless
otherwise noted.) Then I write another animal sonnet called
"Ella the Cat," in which I seek to employ the Rilkean mentality
of "inseeing," unfolding the cat's process of becoming by
re-creating it from within, imagining what I'd feel like if it
were happening to me. Here's part one of my reply:

Konstantin Balmont's "The Panther"

Well made and motley—laggard, hot when sated—
Three days he'll sleep—and afterward, awaking,
Will have a hounding premonition, aching,
The call to hunt! He's growling, agitated.

The tail a-swinging, lazily he goes.
The fur is dappled, and a golden sheen
Will glimmer. Someone noted once the keen
Fine eye's a candle, that uncanny glows.

The pleasant smell of him the air can fill.
The muezzeen, on the steep of Georgian hill,
The panther hymned, who warmest love had won.

As aloe, thickly fragrant, swelled the song:
Snow-leopard singer, he had known him long—
With bloody dusk enflamed, unsettling sun.

It's as if I were saying, "Friend Rainer, you showed me a
psychological portrait of an imprisoned panther in a lyric
with uncommon depth of ontological insight about the fatal
result of being encompassed by unreality, the denial of one's
nature. Now let me show you a panther free, out in the open,
a solar creature radiating heat and the violence and vitality
that go with it." We're having a conversation, as brotherly
as can be. And the sportsmanlike competition is coupled

always with a new dimension of empathy: "And what's more, dear Rainer, I think our fellow pilgrim Konstantin might well become a spiritual friend to us both."

It might even be said that I've invited my two friends to join me in a little comparative literature seminar on panther-presentation. The "muezzin" in the Balmont poem, the one who utters from the minaret, in triumphant singing tones, the glorious call to prayer, is presented as one who has "hymned" the panther, written a lyric poem in its praise. "Unsettling sun" suggests "unsetting sun"—tying in with what I called "violence and vitality," disturbance and deathlessness. The word-play on these two English adjectives won't be found in the Russian original: may I be so bold as to reinvoke my formula, "Translator = Greater"? It may be of interest here to note that one of the greatest translations of all time must surely be Balmont's own rendering of Edgar Allan Poe's "The Bells," which the Russian poet so vastly improved that it could furnish Sergei Rachmaninoff with the libretto for a resplendent symphony-cantata; see my new English version of "Kolokolá" ["The Bells"] by Konstantin Balmont, translated form-faithfully from the Russian in Sergei Rachmaninoff, *The Bells*, opus 35, piano-vocal score, edited with piano reduction by Bruce E. Borton and Timothy M. Rolls (Musica Russica 2016) vii–ix.

As our imaginary seminar continues I'm encouraged to introduce further material to liven up discussion, letting Rilke, Balmont, and me go deeper into the topic of panther-envisionings. The "muezzin" of the above-quoted sonnet, I suggest, is a stand-in for the man who wrote *Wearer of the Panther-Skin*, the great epic poem of medieval Georgia. Balmont, whose translation of this Georgian epic into Russian verse I have read with great pleasure (there is still apparently no verse rendering in English; Balmont's is one of four done into Russian verse). The muezzin can be understood as representing Shota Rustaveli (ca. 1160—after 1220), the supreme poet of Georgia, and his "warmest love" for the panther (or "snow-leopard"—apparently not clearly distinguishable from "panther" in the medieval language), whose own nature appears an emanation of the bloody dusk, the carmine sunset of heroism and hunting, of full-bloodedness and bloody death, intimates the oneness-of-being of panther and poet. We can feel how intensely Balmont, who spent many months with Rustaveli's epic, identifies with the Georgian panther/poet. Here's a sonnet I wrote about Rustaveli, recalling my own travels in the Georgian Republic (*A Lover's Art* poem 105):

Multicultural Love in the Middle Ages:
A Georgian Story

A Russian-speaking study tour. And I'm nineteen.
Today: Tbilisi. It's the year of 'sixty-two.
The thaw is on—all Stalin statues hid from view;
That favored mustache, though, may everywhere be
    seen.

Tall palm trees line the street. Bard Rustaveli knew
This Middle Eastern type of lush, luxuriant scene,
Who told of thwarted lover's wail, travail, and teen
In *Wearer of the Panther Skin*. I'll answer you

About the Georgian language, ev'n before you pose
The question: kin to ancient Hittite. And they chose
The Christian faith, yet in the medieval song

When Tariel has fainted, white-horsed knight and
    strong,
A mullah reads from the Qur'an, reviving him ...
He's off to seek his love, with customary vim.

I might contribute to our imagined seminar discussion further comparative material from my "Virtuoso Translations as Visions of Water and Fire: The Elemental Sublime in Swinburne's Arthurian Tale and Bal'mont's Medieval Georgian Epic," *Modern Language Quarterly* 59 (1998): 410–43. A symposium of poetic siblings will allow an ever-expanding shared intercultural empathy to arise.

Now let's move to part two of my reply to Rilke's "Der Panther," a poem I wrote about the digital photo of a neighbor's cat, sent in an e-mail by my daughter, Sarah Combellick-Bidney:

Ella the Cat

Reclining on her back in playful style,
Near-napping, she is flirting, face half hid
Behind an auburn pillow, where are thrid
Lines white and black, together to beguile

The viewer with her brindled fur where these
Three color-friends a tapestry have made
In tufted weave—or, say, a serenade.
Hind feet part-raised in air, the shadows tease

In dialogue with darker patches. Chin
And cheeks and forepaws lit in snowy tone,
The landscape of her form has emblem grown:
Coquettish pet—sly bliss within.

You'll notice I tried a bit of Rilkean inseeing here, thinking of the half-hidden face behind the pillow as comparable to a lady's partial concealing of her visage by a folding fan at the opera—an attractive strategy of coquettish flirting. The comparisons of the intricately patterned, brindled cat-body to tapestry and landscape suggest good reasons for her proud, quiet joy in the beauty of her gentle, richly-hued form displayed to the photographer.

The two replies taken together offered a supplementary reward for my patient attempt to reproduce the meanings, harmonies, rhythms, and melodic flow of Rilke's panther poem. The song-translation was an act of love, and the conversational double reply was an empathetic way of adding, "Rainer, let's not ever forget your poem: let's keep on con-versing about it and sharing the empathetic joy of unfolding animal personalities in our differing but similar types of metric-melodic portraiture."

Before concluding these prefatory remarks I'd like to offer a sample dialogue in verse from the second Rilke book I translate in this volume, which I'm calling *New Poems II* (*Der neuen Gedichte anderer Teil*, 1908). Rilke's poem that we will look at, another all-time favorite often reprinted, is "Archaic Torso of Apollo" ("Archäischer Torso Apollos"). Corbett writes:

> At some point, we do not know precisely where or when, Rilke came across a statue of Apollo with its head and limbs broken off, and only a naked torso remaining. It may have been a sculpture by Rodin or Michelangelo. Or it may have been the iconic *Belvedere Torso*. Others believe it was the muscular chest of a young Greek man from the ancient city of Miletus, which was on view at the Louvre while Rilke was in Paris. (*C* 208)

In contrast to "The Panther," which traced, from the viewpoint of a captive, the eroding and wasting away of animal reality by (in)human imprisonment, "Archaic Torso" watches vital existence emerge from within a mutilated relic, transcendence lending new being-in-time to the object of a centuries-old near-devastation.

First, the German:

Archäischer Torso Apollos

Wir kannten nicht sein unerhörtes Haupt,
darin die Augenäpfel reihen. Aber
sein Torso glüht noch wie ein Kandelaber,
in dem sein Schauen, nur zurückgeschraubt,

sich hält und glänzt. Sonst könnten nicht der Bug
der Brust dich blenden, und im leisen Drehen
der Lenden könnte nicht ein Lächeln gehen
zu jener Mitte, die die Zeugung trug.

Sonst stünde dieser Stein entstellt und kurz
unter der Schultern durchsichtigem Sturz
und flimmerte nicht so wie Raubtierfelle;

und bräche nicht aus allen seinen Rändern
aus wie ein Stern: denn da ist keine Stelle,
die dich nicht sieht. Du mußt dein Leben ändern.

Next, the translation:

Archaic Torso of Apollo

We had not known of that unheard of head
Where apples of the eyes had ripened, though
His torso's candelabra-like—white glow;
The gaze, half turned away, inhibited,

Yet steady gleams. Not otherwise the bend
Of breast could blinding dazzle, or the loins
In softly turning form a smile that joins
Them to the center that could life expend.

The stone would else be over-short, design
Distorted under shoulders' bright incline,
And glimmer not as fur on beast of prey:

Nor forth could breathe, a burst of stellar ray
From borders all. The seeing shape no strife
Allows evading. You must change your life.

Let's briefly elaborate the dramatic contrast between
"The Panther" and "Archaic Torso of Apollo" in ontological

terms. Non-being, unreality, nothingness—the sole content of the panther's life—turned finally toward a deadness at the center, for we have no real center unless we interact in a way we experience as real with other living beings also felt as real. The sufferers interviewed by ontological psychologist R. D. Laing (*The Divided Self*; *Self and Society*) told him they were "dead" inside because they felt their lives consisted entirely of acting out roles determined by others— roles that had no reality, no meaning, for the individual person considered as a free agent. Unreality is deadness: the experience of extreme non-being, such as the panther had to endure, can be fatal. It is an ontological sickness.

The ontological contrast offered by "Archaic Torso of Apollo" couldn't possibly be greater. The second quatrain and the first tercet—fully half of the poem—explain that even though we no longer see the gaze of the ancient sculptural god-relic, the inward reality it expressed was so intense that it still conditions our response to the torso that remains. The god's super-real gaze, with all its inner richness of being, is expressed today in the dazzle of the manly chest, the smiling of the loins, the length and curvature of the torso, the sharing of the man-nature with the vital predator-beast. Emphatically the speaker affirms that none of these visual effects would be possible without the gaze—which is ontologically super-real though apparently absent in non-being. Non-being, in the form of a spreading infection, ontologically kills the panther; but non-being, in the form of a peril countervailed, makes way for ontological fulfilment in the art work.

How can this be? My experience of the poem tells me that what gave the statue life for the artist, and what resurrects it for the present reader, is the Imaginative Gaze. Imaginative Empathy is the most vital form of Becoming. Life is processual: a human being is the process of its becoming. As active beings who become, we use our Imagination to animate what it sees with potential Becoming which, while being imagined, becomes real Becoming in the spirit of the beholder-imaginer. Becoming changes Nothingness by incorporating it into the reality of process considered as a breathing, a coming-to-be and a passing-away, the breath of life as we know it. For the panther, space-time was gradually contracted and annihilated. For the god-torso, space-time becomes anew, as it was for the artist-imaginer, the realm-act of fulfilling motion, which gives and receives meaning in personal life and in the life of imagination's history. That is the achievement of ontological fulfilment by means of imagining. Such is the power of empathetic imagination that it can (re-) animate with the force of potential Becoming a statue bereft of legs, arms and face. No legs, arms, or face—but it pulsates with the vitality it's empathetically felt to sense arising, bursting forth, within. The widened gaze directed at you is that of the whole torso from olden Greece. Unreality shot to the center to kill the panther. But super-reality (Fr. "surréalité") urges every inch of the archaic statue-body to look at you as if it were a gleaming eye. The diffused body-gaze, without physical eyes, I depict as "half turned away, inhibited"—my attempt to render the German "nur zurückgeschraubt." Literally, the phrase means "only screwed back." I wonder if this idea relates to the Russian "prishchúrennÿe glazá," often translated as a "screwing up" of the eyes. There's an essay where Edmund Wilson talks about this half-withdrawn look of characters, involving a kind of eye movement common in Russian novels and in Russia, but which he has not seen in other countries.

Indeed, a surreal face may more clearly emerge the longer we look: while the gaze of unviewed "eyes" will now perfuse the body entire, a "smile" is relocated to the life-giving loins. Strangest of all, perhaps, even the panther's gleaming "fur" has been teleported. The "fur on beast of prey" edges our Apollo in the direction of Dionysus, to whom panthers were holy. Crucial words—"white," "glow," "gleams," "dazzle," "blinding," "bright," "candelabra," "stellar"—turn stone to fire. Like Balmont's panther in Georgia, the torso is a creature of sun.

Perhaps nearly everyone who today tours "ancient" Greece feels obliged to practice, so far as can be managed, the kind of transformative observation the German poet teaches here. I took a pair of two-week antiquarian tours, one of Greece and one of Egypt; and they were as different as could be. Masterworks of Egyptian funerary art retain the vivid colors of their earth-based paints in caves and tombs after the passing of millennia. But Grecian architectural monuments are, too often, mere ravaged remnants of their former glory—sometimes little more than a pile of rubble (even if surrounded by a breathtakingly vast panorama of fields and wooded hills). Double-view postcards offer the tourist a short course in Rilkean reimagining. The card will show, from one angle, some rough-hewn rocks, but from another angle we behold a lovely structure vividly re-pictured by an archeologically well-schooled present-day imaginative painter.

Rilke's fiery metamorphosing of ancient Greek art stands in contrast to the kind of idealizing re-vision offered in the golden age of romantic German philhellenism. Johann Joachim Winckelmann (1717–1768), inventor of modern art history, set the tone for attitudes toward Greek sculpture that flourished during the Age of Goethe, as when Hegel in his *Lectures on Aesthetics* declares ancient Hellenic art a perfect union of spirit and body. (My esteemed teacher, the late Erich Heller, in one of his lectures called Hegel "the theologian of the German nostalgia for Greece.") Winckelmann summed up the distinctive Hellenic achievement by claiming that the ancient statues had "noble simplicity" and "quiet grandeur" ("edle Einfalt," "stille Größe"). Rather than seethe with a perfusing vital beast-like fire, they're noble, simple, quiet, and majestic. Evidently the pallor of the marble helped produce for Winckelmann a calming, cooling mood. Subsequent research, though, has made abundantly clear the tendency of the Greeks to paint their sculpture in dramatic, vital colors; and this ontological promotion—added life, richer being—is portrayed on the double-view postcards I mentioned.

Nonetheless, Winckelmann, like Rilke, was a poetic visionary of a high order, and if his prose poems are read with the empathy of a skilled (and psychoanalytically alert) translator we find ourselves enchantedly afloat on ancient oceans. Here is Alex Potts in *Flesh and the Ideal: Winckelmann and the Origins of Art History* (Yale, 2000) 171–172, citing Winckelmann, *Geschichte der Kunst des Alterthums* (Vienna, 1776) 163:

> The Laocoön is condensed into an image of "muscles ... that lie like hills, flowing into one another," the [Belvedere] Torso of ones "that are like the surge of waves on a calm sea, rising in a flowing relief, and moving in a gently changing swell," and the [Belvedere] Apollo of ones that are "supple, and blown like molten glass in hardly visible undulations that are more apparent to the feeling than to the sight." Seen in this quasi-connoisseurial mode, these complex figures are made into fetishized objects. They are in effect each reduced to an immaculately formed inanimate surface, which shows not the least hint of disjunction or tension, but at the same time might intimate a potentially disturbing suppressed charge, as in the image of the gently swelling [maternal] sea conjured up by the Belvedere Torso. ... The suggested dissolution of fixed form in flowing contour fosters a "narcissistic" fantasy in which the recalcitrant externality of the sculptural objects melts away and seems to be modulated to the subtlest stirrings of the viewer's desire. (cited in Bidney, "Peace and Pathos in the Epiphanies of Rupert Brooke: Contours of Narcissistic Desire," *English Literature in Transition: 1880–1920* 48.3 [2005]: 325)

My way of responding in dialogue is to compare Winckelmann's water sculptures (octet, first two quatrains) to the fiery one of Rilke (sestet, final two tercets):

Reply

The noble, simple, quiet grandeur found
When Winckelmann a statue would observe
Depended on perception of the curve
Recalling swelling seas no man would sound.

That roundness had a sweet maternal ease
Where bounty of the ocean would abound;
The bodies molten seemed: each contour wound
In smoothened surging, soothing urgencies.

See, here, the gleam and dazzle and the star,
The candelabrum and the glimmering?
The water-mother turned to fiery king.

The statue and the god have been remanned.
We hear the silent strike of a command:
Arise, and be as the eternal are.

A familiar excitement returns to me: we're holding a
heaven-seminar where Winckelmann, Potts, and Rilke share
with me an empathetic and spirited colloquy that takes
account of the never-ending variety of elemental epiphanic
transformation. My style pays homage to that of Rilke, whom
I dearly love—I hope he smiles when reading of "smoothened
surging, soothing urgencies."

I pay additional homage to him in my final verse, which
alludes to the last two-liner of Shelley's elegy: "The soul of
Adonais, like a star, / Beacons from the abode where the
eternal are." Adonais, blending Hebrew Adonai with Greek
Adonis, is the poet's mythic presentation of his dead but
resurrected friend John Keats in the form of an ancient-
modern fertility spirit. A supreme ontological promotion—yet
worthily rivaled by the Rilkean ravaged, crafted stone that

looks at you with its godly body and issues the command, Be born again.

Thank you for visiting my workshop, and welcome now to 178 dialogues containing 356 lyrics bringing together 1907–8 and 2017 with the help of publishers in Leipzig, Germany and Vestal, New York.

NEW POEMS I,
TRANSLATED WITH
VERSE REPLIES

(1) Early Apollo

Through twigs how often, yet ungarlanded
With leafage, dawn appears: for him 'twould seem
That spring is here: and so, within his head
No obstacle would yet prevent the gleam

Of lyrics that might nearly strike one dead—
But in his look, no shadow met the eyes:
Too cool for bay, the temples, we'd have said—
And only later from the brow will rise

A garden, long-stemmed roses, fine to see,
From which the single leaves, when they shall fall,
About the trembling mouth will driven be

That yet is silent, and untried, and shines,
And only with his smile it drinks, divines
A singing flowing in, awaiting all.

(1) Reply

As Adam dreamed of Eve in Milton-lines,
May we surmise the growing god when young
Might smiling prophesy the high designs
Kind fate may hold in store? That silent tongue

Will Hermes liven when a shell upflung
By ocean to the shore he redefines:
When it with sinews tight is newly strung,
Behold the lyre! The boy his columbines

And asphodel and amaranth entwines
In idle play, but when will he have sung
To harmony of harp? We find no signs

He ever tried, still rummaging among
Some floral toys. Each moment he enshrines.
O lucky youth, to whom no duties clung!

(2) Young Woman's Lament

How we liked alone to be
While we still were children; we
Found it mild, the solitude.
Some in struggle must abide;
Others may remain aside,
Staying near, or straying wide—
Path, and pet, and picture-mood.

Then I thought, life cannot cease
Lending solitude-release:
By ourselves are we beguiled.
Isn't inner life the best?
Is it not the comfort-test:
Comprehending as a child?

I've rejected been of late:
Now to burden over-great
My reclusive life has grown
While upon my swelling breast
Feeling stands, at wing-behest,
And for flight, or end, I moan.

(2) Reply

Caterpillar, on a leaf,
Can recall your mother's grief—
So the thought of William Blake.
But the child must mourn as well,
Half-rejoicing in the spell
That portends a major break.

Biologic hormone growth
Means that we are nothing loth
Prospect new in life to try.
Trial by ordeal indeed
Though it be, occasion heed
Lest your fate should pass you by.

Liminals in later age
Are a harder thing to gauge.
What is butterfly in me?
Part is gift and part my will
Living-mission to fulfill,
Swinging on a leaf, I see.

(3) Love Song

How can I so hold back my soul, that it
Will not be touching yours? And how shall I
Upheave it over you to other things?
Oh, how I'd wish to take it, make it fit
Near something lost in dark that downward brings,
Deep in an alien quiet place to lie,
Unswaying when your deepness, even, swings.
But everything that touches you and me
Takes us together, unifyingly,
Two notes, one tone, in single bow-stroke fleet.
Upon what instrument our stringing? and
Of whom the holding violinist-hand?
O song, O sweet.

(3) **Reply**

for Sarah

A song can, buried wordless, yet be hid
Until, emerging to a springtime sky,
It upward bubbles in a cooling rill
With freshness undiminished. So it did
Within my daughter's mind, who heard it still,
Forgotten meaning having long gone by.
She telephoned, and asked, but memory
The words abandoned had, as well, in me.
The title, though, with apt computer aid,
Would let her soon rebuild it, and she sang
The melody at seder. Risen gift!
From underground, the Mósheh tones uplift.
They rose, they rang.

(4) Eranna to Sappho

O! you wild wide-ranging thrower-girl:
Like a spear, one more still thing,
'Mid my kin I lay. But one who'd sing
Threw me far. Where *am* I, head awhirl?
Me can no one homeward bring.

Sisters think of me, weave warp and weft:
Well-known treadings fill a house at rest.
I alone am distant, I have left,
All atremble, mere request;
For the goddess here, the loveliest,
Leads my life, myth-glowing she, the blest.

(4) Reply

Thunder of the trumpets of the night
Came to me: on steed of god
Pounding unabated dream-hard sod
One who bringing bliss in part affright
Prophesied of dawning awed.

Then I saw the water where the sun
Nets invented made of liquid ray,
Wove in heart what dark had but begun,
Now to throw me woken into day
Purpose brave euterpal to portray:
Be horizon-light; arise, and run!

(5) Sappho to Eranna

You I would disquiet bring
And, a staff enwound, would swing,
Deathlike you would I perfuse,
Grant you to the grave, to lose
Self in All, each several thing.

(5) Reply

Named *Mainádes*, they who rave
Thyrses aimed and rocks would lave.
Rhabdomancer Bassarid,
Milk and honey drinking, hid
Deadly strength in wonder wave.

(6) Sappho to Alkaios

fragment

And what might you have wished to say to me—
Approach my spirit, do you think you can?
With hiding eyes, cast down so timidly
Before the never said, so near. O man,

You realize the telling of these things
Tore us apart, with glory all too free.
I'm thinking: being with you men—it brings
The ruin of our sweet virginity,

Which we—both I, the knowing one, and they
Who know as I—from god have guarded well,
Maintained intact, so Mytilenë may
As by an orchard-rich aroma-spell
Convey the fragrance of our growing breasts—.

Ah yes, indeed the breasts that you did not
Select as for a fruit festoon, O you
Suitor with face yet turned away in thought.
Abandon me, and go; then maybe through
My lyre may come what's lacking, unforgot.

This god the helper cannot be of two,
But should he pass through *one*, there may be
    wrought

- - - - - - - - - - - - - - -

(6) Reply

He seems to have enough *Bescheidenheit*,
Shy lover, with a face he turns away ...
Would it be more divine for *Dreistigkeit*
To rise, and bring the fragrance into play?

She looked with favor on the senses' lore
(Perhaps Eranna has more amplitude?);
She's guarded from the gods, will yet outpour
A godlike love through lyre by god endued.

They both at Kallistheia hymns had read,
And ancient commentators have assessed
The competition. Who came out ahead?
Depends on what criteria were best.
His range is wide, hers narrow. Let it rest ...

The tenth of muses Plato called her. He
Would like a thinner flaming's higher climb.
She loved intensely. To divinity,
Intent upon her lyre-escape from time,
She might desire by tune to be removed.

What trouble-creature: double-tending, we,
Who comprehended less than we had loved

- - - - - - - - - - - - - - -

(7) Tombstone of a Young Woman

We yet recall her. As if all must be
Recurrent, into an eternity.

As if on lemon-coast you were a tree,
Your small light breasts you bore, so gracefully,
Toward the rushing of his blood, where he—

That god ...
                    And you would gladly to the slender
Elusive pamperer of women bow,
The sweet, the glowing, warm as thought, as tender,
Who, overshadowing your thigh would now
Incline, as gentle as your bending brow.

(7) Reply

We love the god. Who don't, deny their blood
And come to grief. Not so, who go to greet.

As Adam is a fire immixed with mud,
Of whom the jinns are jealous, let the flood,
Bright water, drowsy wine, a heady sweet,

Endear ...
        The deity let meet the maid.
We love their beauty. So the synonym
Of beautiful is "lovely." Unafraid
Of grace and justice (both are "fair") arrayed
In splendor, Spirit bows: to her, to him.

(8) Offering

How my body blooms from every vein,
More aroma'd, now I'm knowing you;
Better gait and slenderness I gain ...
You await: who *are* you? tell me true.

Look: I feel I've left myself behind,
Losing oldness, like the leaves that fell;
In your smile a pure-eyed star I find
Over you, soon over me as well.

All that can through childhood years aware
Nameless and like water purely gleam
After you I name at altar fair
That I see enkindled by your hair,
Coronated by your breasts in dream.

(8) Reply

Praise to brilliance: waning waves have gone
Since I felt aurora'd, aura'd, or
Leaf-enwreathed when petal-shower shone:
Former âge *d'or* that I adore.

Let me, ever awed, belaud the more
What will comfort yet the lover wan:
Staying flagon, harvest-wagon store,
Goddess cornucopial at dawn.

Drops of mercy dew bedeck the lawn;
Ámor says to Roma, Troy restore!
Helen-tresses flowing, borne upon
Winds they kindle, passion carry on:
This the only flame we're waiting for.

(9) Eastern Song of Day

Won't it remind you of a coast, our bed,
A strip of shoreline stretching where we lie?
Of nothing I'm more sure, my feelings led
To fainting trance-life by your bosom high.

This night, its many cries, you will allow,
With all the animals that claw and call—
It is not odd to point of horror? How?
What we name day, slow rising past the pall—
Can we then better comprehend it now?

We have to lie as tightly clasped together
As flower petals 'round an ashen urn:
For all is measureless, regardless whether
The heaped uprushing ills toward us turn.

But while we hug each other clingingly
So's not to view what terror heads our way,
A something may be stirred in you, in me:
We cannot live unless we both betray.

(9) Reply

There is a love that makes the lover small.
There is an egotism framed for two.
There is a menace which an inward crawl
Will motivate, an ingrown me-and-you.

Distinctions will in fading vision blur
When con*vers*ation has no other aim
But one together-turning, circular,
A yang and yin within a shrinking frame
That tightly coiling joys in time prefer.

The vertebrae get slighter as we age
And fuse and limit movement as we go.
Twin yearning may suffice to keep the rage
Of nature still, and fear may hide the foe.

What measure will distinguish poetry
From lunacy? The presence of a friend.
But lest you shrink to group of two or three
Be sure your friendship circle to extend.

(10) Abishag

I

She lay. Her child-arms placed by servants were
To clasp the aged fading one around
On whom she lay, the sweet long hours, bound—
Worried that he, so aged, might demur.

And she would turn her face within his beard,
At times, when suddenly an owl would cry;
And all that was the night, and that she feared
And longed for would assemble, standing by.

The stars kept trembling, ev'n as she would do;
A breeze went seeking through the sleeping room;
The curtain stirred, a sign one might pursue;
Her gaze would trace it back into the gloom.

Yet clung she, holding to the dark one, old,
And, unaffected by the chosen night,
Lay on his princely majesty, so cold,
In virgin wise, and with her spirit light.

II

The monarch sat, reviewed the empty day
Of deeds he'd done, how unfelt pleasures weigh;
The dog, pet cherished in a loving way—.
But Abishag, at evening, yet would stay
Above him curved. His muddled life—it lay
Abandoned as the coasts, dire peril-test,
Below the star-frame of her quiet breast.

And he at times, who women well apprised,
Beneath his bending eyebrows recognized
The moveless mouth, of kiss incapable;
He saw: her feelings' withe did not extend
Its green to meet his depth, of longing full.
That chilled him. Like a harking hound he'd lend
His thought to seeking self, blood's final pull.

(10) Reply

My father was more quiet every day.
No pain he felt, he said, but simply lay
In contemplation, calm, a Socrates,
And rarely would he speak, yet seemed at ease.
He liked to hear me read the psalms, a few.
Before, I'd read him stories that were new:
Tolstóy, Shalom Aleikhem, warm and wise—
A gentle pleasure in his quiet eyes.

Each day the silence grew, the sleep increased,
Until the waking hours had nearly ceased.
He then requested what would prove to be
A final reading of Psalm Twenty-Three.
I finished it, and put the book aside;
I heard him saying, Take me. And he died.

(11) David Sings Before Saul

I

Monarch, do you hear my string-play spell
Throwing forth the distances we gain?
Stars come rushing, crazy in the main,
And we fall at last as falling rain,
Then a blossom where the raindrops fell.

Maidens blossom; well you ken their fates.
They, seducing me, are women now;
Virgin fragrance feel—to which we bow;
Youths are waiting, tensed, they know not how,
Slender, breathing at the silent gates.

I to bring this back to you desire—
Drunken, though, the tumult of my tone:
And your nights, O King, your nights I moan,—
For what then you formed in passion-fire—
O, how lovely had those bodies grown!

I am faithful to your memory;
Hints, I get. And yet what strings can be
Right for capturing their longing-groan?—

II

King, I ask that you, who this could take,
And who've overshadowed me with force
And with ripest life have changed my course,
From your throne come down at last and break
This my lyre you've weakened—no remorse.

It is like a tree that's hauled away:
Through the boughs that fruits had borne for you,
Deeps of coming days are showing through
That I cannot grasp; what can I say ...

Let me sleep no longer near my lyre;
Look upon the youthful hand: a man
Stands, O King; the strength will he acquire
That to grasp the body-octaves can?

III

King, you in obscurity would hide,
Yet you're in my power after all.
Strong my song, not ripped, not riven wide;
Cold, the space between us will appall.
Mine the orphaned heart, yours the confounded,
Hang in clouds of anger you have sounded;
Raging, mutual, the bites abide,
Clawing, clutched, becoming one in gall.

Can't you feel how we've each other bound?
King, O King, the weight has spirit found:
When we onto one another hold,
You to youth, O King, I to the old—
Single constellation circling 'round!

(11) Reply

Enemies each other mirror. Dread
Are the love in heart and hate in head
When the two unending, blended, more
Venomed grow and gravely interpour.
Stifled must desire to struggle come
Muffled when respect has struck it dumb.

God His image can in man create,
Yet the latter zeal may feel abate
When a person who, the deity-
Place usurping, urges, Be like me.
Should the youth-compeller strive at war
With *himself* as well, what woe in store!

Twin the images that intermix,
Widened split had crisis come to fix.
If the rebel truce too soon declare,
Phantom mind-abuse in youth will flare
Till the spent seceder be laid waste,
Hades-bent in suicidal haste.

Double is the barely conscious blight:
Manichee-ideals, implanted, fight.
Youth, who'd be two things at once, will get
Fever from the twins in conflict set.
Four the foes; the two in youthful mind,
Two in elder's, hope to hell consigned.

(12) Joshua Speaks to the People

As when a dam by stream is overflowed
And broken through by disemboguing mass,
So breached the bulwark of the oldest class
The voice of Joshua, the final goad.

Oh how the strong were smitten who had laughed;
How wrung, the hands and heart of every man;
Like thirty battles' tone-rise fore and aft,
The single voice, and now that voice began.

Again the myriads with amazement filled
As on the fateful day of Jericho—
But now the trumpets were in him instilled,
The walls of all their lives were swaying so

That they were rolling, with a horror pregnant,
And unprotected, overwhelmed until
They thought, recalled, how he, the mighty, regnant,
At Gibeon had told the sun, Be still.

And God, withdrawn, appeared a servant scared,
And grabbed the sun until He hurt His hands
To favor thus the battle as it fared
Because a single man had made demands.

And that's the man, whom every spirit hears;
They'd thought that in his ancient age immense
He'd weigh but little—ten-past-hundred years—
But viewed him standing, shattering their tents.

He proved the hail that down on grass blades
    rushed:
What would you promise God? You can't refuse
Demands of gods unnumbered: you must choose.
Yet, choose away: by God you'll still be crushed.

And then—unprecedented haughtiness:
I and my house, we're married to Him—yes.

Then cried they all: O help us, give a sign!
And strengthen us for choosing the Divine.

But they beheld him silent as for years
He'd been; in mountain town he disappears.
And then—no more. That was the final time.

(12) Reply

Sweet, hurtful—the Supreme of honeybees.
The deities reflect their worshipers.
So Joshua the hothead god bestirs,
Though, heated-fingered, He may feel unease.

Four hundred ninety—that is quite a lot
Of times the Jesus hearer must forgive
A sinner. Yet the Tyrant, fugitive,
Returns to burn the world, Lord unforgot.

So Jung would try to show (*Reply to Job*)
The Jesus-writ in dream-work redesigned
To show a split within the growing mind;
Two deities each other's weakness probe.

Split psyche in the writer? Fighting gods.
The Byron who was lauding Nature calm
Confronts a deity without a qualm
In "Manfred" to defy the cosmic odds.

What's "god"? To call upon, invoke, implore,
Deriving from the Sanskrit root of *hu*,
Appears to be what I'm alluding to.
Deep calls to deep, of depth to mirror more.

How best to picture Him, or image Her?
Claim Swedenborg and Blake: no cloud of light
Profoundly will convey to human sight
The meta-phor to bear you. They prefer

The following: the best that you have known
In human virtue and pre-eminence
Imagine made yet greater, made immense,
Made infinite, to scope of heaven grown.

The Pseudo-Denys Areopagite
Declared all god-talk purely metaphor,
Approximation, faulty, only door
To open on the Dark Beyond Our Light.

(13) The Departure of the Lost Son

To leave, now, all bewildered-making things
That, though our own, to us do not belong,
That, like the water in the ancient springs,
Lend shaken mirror, get our image wrong;
From all of this, that stubbornly yet clings
Like thorns, to fare into the distance dim,
And this, and him,
Whom one no more could see
(So daily they'd become, habitual)
Gently to view, of reconcilement full,
As if beginning, and quite near to be,
And getting hints of how impersonal
The woe was, over all, and constantly,
The sorrow childhood bonds had loaded, and
To leave again, unloosing then one's hand,
As if in new-healed wound more salt were thrown,
And travel on: but where? To what's unknown,
Far, to an unrelated, warmer land,
Behind all action, gray coulisse-wing, grown
Indifferent, whether garden, or a wall,
And then go on: and why? Urge, inclination,
Or stubbornness, or dark-hued expectation:

To take this on yourself, in vain
Perhaps to let what you had held fall by,
And die alone, not comprehending why—

Is that the way, new life in time to gain?

(13) Reply

You'll have to get the strength to be a sun.
The red in bloodscrim on the heav'n portrays
Adonis gone whenever day is done
And so the human-fateful hue displays.
Don't claim the race we run
Dismays. For what we're prophesied to lack
Is coming back
And filling vein and artery; the heart
In tensing, then relaxing, tells the brain
A Way of Alternation so to gain:
The spring, the flood, of measured time and art.
The hardest part:
To sacrifice applause, which not for naught
Will rhyme with laws. Nor let the mind be caught
In others' fear that would the god constrain.
They'd crudely soothe a crucifixion-pain:
Too hot, the warming warns. Till yonder dust
Come nigh, keep well alive the wanderlust:
Benumbing comfort is the greater strain.
We ponder must
The way to keep astir. For loss and gain
To singer are the burden, the refrain.

Of Nothing, bear the brunt.
We Beckett-bold the wreck it holds confront.
Recall the god who daily dies

And so the heaven both defies and deifies.

(14) The Garden of Olives

He upward went among the leafage gray,
All gray and spreading in the olive-lands,
A dusty brow down wearily to lay
Deep in the dustiness of heated hands.

Nothing but this. And it has been the end.
Here must I go, still onward, ever blind;
And why that message tell me yet to send:
You are—when You no longer can I find?

I can no longer find You. Not in me.
Not in the others, or this rock I see.
Find You no more. Alone—yes, utterly:

I am alone with all the human fear
That I, through You, had hoped to lighten here,
Who *are not*. Shame unnamable and drear.

Later they'd say: an angel would appear.

But why an angel? No, there came the night
And rummaged mindlessly among the leaves,
Disciples troubling with a dream that grieves.
So why an angel? No, there came the night.

The night was none that we in mind may keep;
Like many hundreds going by.
The dogs were sleeping, and the rock asleep.
An ordinary night, to make one weep,
That waited, till the morning rise on high.

No angels will arrive for such entreater,
Surrounding nights are not for this made great.
The lost-to-self no sorrow-cure will sate.
Their fathers left them, they will view no greeter;
No mothers' laps in comfort them await.

(14) Reply

I am the way, the truth, the life, the light,
Said Jesus, and the pupils followed him.
But grim the horrid rustling grove at night
Where hope is silenced and the prospect dim.
I'm minded of the sufferer Hallāj,
Who claimed, I am the truth, as Jesus had.
Like Prophet-ladder on the great mirāj,
The goal was high—and yet the ending sad.

The Christ was crucified, the martyr killed;
Yet daring faith flared on, as saints had willed:
Each life, desire in skiey fire instilled.

Their dying, call not tragic—all will die.
The upper star was Christ, and love is why.
Hallāj—a spark of light in Allah's eye.

Bright minds beam light when they from bodies fly.

(15) Pietà

So, Jesus, here again I see your feet,
The feet of one so youthful then, and bare
When I'd undressed them, washed them tenderly;
They stood all tangled in my outspread hair:
White deer in thornbush, they appeared to me.

Your limbs, the never-loved, I see them, sweet
Within this night of love that we would greet.
We never down together lay. No more
To do but, now, be wakeful and adore.

Your hands, Beloved: see them, they are torn
By wounds that from no bite of mine were born.
Your heart is open: one may enter in,
Though mine alone the entry might have been.

Now you are wearied, and your lips desire
No more can feel for mine, that ache entire—.
O Jesus, when was it our time? Now far ...
We both in wondrous way quite ruined are.

(15) Reply

The Mary who had washed the leader's feet
And Mary Magdalen, who'd been the first
To see him when the bonds of death he'd burst,
Devoted servants both, a guerdon meet
Had well received when those no more immersed

In social doctrines of the time of Paul
That asked the women not to speak at all
In church, but live beneath "obedience,"
The prohibition ended. We're less tense.

Of Magdalen a gospel one composed;
For centuries it languished undisclosed.
That Christ of her a spirit-comrade made
So high in rank St. Peter had dismayed.

The Gnostic often lent a higher place
To women prophets than the orthodox
Had done, like Peter fearing losing face.
But time moves on and heaven-gate unlocks.

(16) Song of the Women to the Poet

Look how all things are opened: so are we;
For we are nothing but such blessed state.
What blood and darkness was in beast would wait
In us to grow to spirit and to be

Our farther spirit-cry. To you it cries.
Into your face you take it, to be sure,
As 'twere a landscape: calm, uneager, wise.
And that is why we think perhaps that you're

Not what we cry to. Yet, are you not he
To whom we'd lose ourselves? And how could we
Be in another being something *more*?

With us, the endless wanders on, you see.
But *be*, you lips, that we may hear its lore;
You, Sayer-of-us, be, we pray you: be.

(16) Reply

The women so evoke my empathy!
Of Allah had the Prophet said that He
The breast of those well favored would expand
To the Surrender. Who's the god at hand?

The poet, turner to eternity
Of what to seeker flashes fleetingly?
Yet *lastingness* and *value* to equate
Will dubious equivalencies mate.

I wrote about my father's tranquil death
Yet cannot claim I grant him endless breath.
A poet-savior? No. Duration's fine,
But less than vital to our soul-design.

His life was worth what it had come to be.
The merit of it can't depend on me.
To be is not to be perceived, be read.
His value: far beyond what can be said.

(17) The Death of a Poet

He lay. His upturned countenance, yet clear,
Pale, on the high-piled pillows, would deny,
Since all the world and all his knowing why
Were torn away from senses, ear and eye;
The face fell back on the indifferent year.

Not one who saw him living ever knew
How fully he was one with all of this;
The deep and meadow, every water-bliss—
They *were* his face, yet more than one could view.

And oh, the face was all that, ranging, wide,
Would fain be near to him, for favor sue;
The mask that wastes in fear and pales in rue
Is tender, open as the inner side
Of fruit, that in the air is ruined, too.

(17) Reply: André Bjerke's "Rainer Maria Rilke"

*translated from Alexander Schlayer's German
rendering of the Norwegian*

His word is wrapt in wider mantle made
Of quiet, as a garden under snow—
Fed by deep rills alone! And yet I know,
See, under verbal skin, thin veins displayed.

Poetry is, for him, news from the land
Within, as though inside a bloom there stood
An almond tree, to demonstrate what would
Come from an Unknown God's own magic hand.

Before such word, that spirit-light shone through,
Like mountain crystal by the strength of sun
Perfused, the others pale and fade within.

Here radiates the image viewed anew:
So juices through the purest fruit-flesh run
From a fresh cut, and overspread the skin.

(18) Buddha

As if he hearkened. Quiet: what is far ...
We stop, hold back, don't hear it anymore.
A star is he. And every other star—
Those we don't see—stand 'round about him. For—

Oh—he is all. And we, why should we wait
For him to see us? Had he lack, or need?
Were we to bow before him here, indeed,
He would stay deep, in beastlike-heavy state.

And what us humbly to his feet would move
A myriad of years within him wheels.
He has forgotten what our species feels
And what he feels will us reprove.

(18) Reply

The wakened Buddha's rare and perfect peace
Could never be available to me:
The semi-empty sempiternity,
De-spiring, feels a breathing nearly cease.

The nearest I may come to that release
From seething life dissevered cannot be
Entirely, yet because I would be free
The awed nirvana-calm of early Greece,

Though from afar, in starlike shine to know
In heart, my breath below the Tree of Bo
Will, with an empathy enlarging, slow

As of a cat asleep. Of OM the O
Is A and U combined, Out-In, the M
A time-eliding line uniting them.

(19) The Angel of the Meridian

Chartres

'Round the cathedral when the storm bursts free—
Plunging denier who relentless broods—
We all at once will feel more tenderly
Inclined to you, your smile, your lighter moods.

You, figure lending feeling, light in smile,
Whose mouth is hundred mouths' collected powers:
You've no idea how we slide our hours
Away from happy height of sunny dial

On which the parts entire of all the day,
All equal, stand alike in balance deep,
As if all hours were ripe in rich array.

What of our being do you know, you stone?
More blessed-faced, can you then hold, and keep,
That tablet with you into night, alone?

(19) Reply

The angel of the happy southern smile
Is the reflection of a human sun
That with a storm would rather soon be done
And contemplate the ample light awhile

Than dream of northern dark and malison.
But that's our paradox: we make of stone
A mirror-cheer, a love-note Mayward flown,
The opposite of hard, for that's no fun.

A fountain climbs that would in nature fall.
We scrape the sky with daring buildings tall
That dwarf the might they're meant to magnify.

Mount Rushmore'd presidential death deny.
Rock-pyramid with effort large a small
Constructor mocked when I would pass them by.

(20) The Cathedral

Within those little hamlets where, around,
The houses crouch as at a country fair,
One of a sudden saw: with frightened air,
He shut the booths and quieted the sound
Of criers, and the drumming put on hold,
And listened upward with alerted ear—:
While tranquilly as always in the old
And folded buttress-mantle would appear
Cathedral, of the houses knowing naught.

Within each little hamlet you can see
How far above what the surroundings brought
Soared the cathedrals, high uprising, free,
Transcending, as the nearness all too great
Of daily life will overclimb the sight,
So there'd be nothing else, as if 'twere Fate
Inside them lifted to immensity,
Turned stone, a thing perdurable to make,
And not what in a darkened lane they'd see
That random labels made by chance would take
And go along, as children green and red—
What shops had offered—for their outfits wore.
In areas low-lying all the more
Was birth of strength and striving, high intent,
And love was handed 'round like wine and bread,
And portals pouring forth a love lament,
Life wavering in what the hour-bell said;
And in the tow'rs, filled with relinquishment,
That of a sudden rose no more—death led.

(20) Reply

So were we early in our schooldays taught:
The body faded, soul gained heaven-size,
The rising of a world-transcending thought
Wiping the tears forever from our eyes.
Feng shui, however, claimed a steeple-spear
Would cleave a landscape with a warlike thrust.
We have a trouble-causing conflict here:
The curving slope of the pagoda must
Make Gothic waver: can our thought cohere?

A piercing jab? But Steiner claims a curve
Is calming: corner, angle need be masked
With curtain, softened lighting. And Gaudí
Soft-rounded furniture the craftsmen tasked
With building, far more comforting. A swerve,
A dome, a circle—perfect, are they not?
Parmenidean Being's round, and we
May like the rhyme of womb and room. Forgot
In Gothic talk is Caracalla's dome:
Penn Station copied it, far more like home
Than spire and out-of-sighting of the mind
To seek what none on planet earth may find:
A Something that cessation of the breath
Requires, the Allegory of the Cave
That Plato wrote made clear. And so to death
"High" logic will our aspiration lead.
We've always wanted more, too much indeed.
A modesty of aim befits the brave
Who now, without apocalypse, would save
Our sibling creatures with undaunted speed.

(21) The Portal

I

There they remained, as if the flood, the chute,
Moved back again, whereof the surge in throes
Washed all these stones, till they from wave arose;
In falling, from their hands an attribute

The waters took, the hands that far too kind
And giving were, to hold an object fast.
Basaltic forms from current-swell, at last,
We haloed, severed, bishop-blest will find;

Protection came in trials for awhile
By guard of tranquil hours, the face, the smile
Preserved on quiet clock tow'r looking down;

Retreating now behind the empty gate
Won't roaring shell-sounds for an ear abate—
They had begun the moaning in the town.

II

In this, how great the breadth that will outspread,
As in and by coulisses of a scene
The world is meant; the hero's cloak-folds mean
A hid capacity for deeds ahead:—

So came the darkness of this gate, to fling
Up from its depth a tragic drama-swell;
From Father-God will so the strength upwell,
Both powers marvelously altering,

A Son becoming, though divided here
In small and near-unspeaking roles, so kind,
Constructed from what misery'd begun.

For only thus can rise (let this be clear)
From castaways, and from the mad and blind,
The Savior as the only actor, One.

III

So they arise, and to the hearts adhere
(They stand forever; they will never go);
From clothing-folds alone may there appear
A gesture as austere as these; ev'n so

They will, stride half completed, standing be—
While centuries the statues overtake—
And, balanced on supporting corbel, make
A place within a world they cannot see,

Confusion-world (they'd little known of that),
Beast, figure (seeming perilous, in fact)
That bend and shake, maintained amid it all,

For every figure, like an acrobat,
Appears convulsive, will so wildly act,
That never dust upon its brow may fall.

(21) Reply

I

My poet cousin, medieval friend
Is Rainer, for as here we see him, free
And burdened, all the whirling urgent three
Ideals he kept well balanced, could extend

Skilled hand and wit, a juggler and *jongleur,*
His blood astir with goodness, beauty, truth,
A depth of age, a bloomingness of youth
Enlisting, him in noble sport to spur

The spheres (each with a center everywhere)
To keep afloat: they never wholly merge
(Dimmed unity that Dante on the verge

Made mutely fail), yet neither fear nor care
May countermand the heart-cathartic purge
When in the *saltimbanque* the soul will surge.

II

The hero wants a monument—the saint
(Too humble thus to name himself) must needs
Be carven, painted, so his flame-born deeds,
The glory of the savior-story, mayn't

Have vanished, or be banished, faded, faint.
What's more, the Lord made jesters; one who feeds
The humor-hunger room will open, heeds
The incongruity that God no taint

Considered but the world with it endued
To serve the principle of plenitude.
At burning forest or at ruined Troy

Though Homer may have wept, a royal joy
To him now blinded, bowed, had yet accrued.
If Jesus cried, the lyre is Hermes' toy.

III

The poet, scientist, and saint combine
Their effort to advance humanity.
Yet candor grants to him *antinomy*
As aid who'd gladly fathom a design.

Philosophy can't reconcile the three
Nor Einstein, Jesus, Rembrandt can align
In single path zodiacal, with sign
Completing sign in happy syzygy.

Bacchantic Daimon-fire will, mantic, we
With Hegel and with Rumi gladly see.
Be Goethe-Háfiz candle: waste away

Yet radiate with gratitude, and say:
By energy that conflict cannot shun
Make every act determined, dared, and done.

(22) Rose Window

Within: their paws, with slow and lazy tread,
Create a quiet made bewildering:
And then one cat—how suddenly!—is led
Upon the other wand'ring cat to fling

A pow'rful glance: great eye will take it in—
That glance, which from a whirlpool-center grows,
Controlled—and but a little while will swim,
And then sink down; of world no more it knows.

And yet the eye that seemed to rest and nod
Now opens, blinking, and in frenzy glows
And rips, red-blooded, deep into the foe—:

From a cathedral's darkness-being so
Will grip the heart an ample window-rose
And violently rip it into God.

(22) Reply

We heard of love-bites on the Christ,
Now learn of catfights in the rose.
By vivid images enticed
The poet is: the passion glows.

With dissonance a highly spiced
Aroma, pungent savor goes;
They well convey the work of *Geist*
By what the God-seized body knows.

Sense-pleasure will the singer heist
From what the anchorite deemed foes
That far from temple porticoes

Appeared to live. But love! It sows
Within the heart what light sufficed
For grand Damascan overthrows.

(23) The Capital

As from the progeny of dream that night
Brought forth tormenting and bewildering,
So wakes the day, from capital to fling
The vaulted armature in seeming flight

And leave, oppressed and swallowed riddlingly,
The hidden creatures with the wings that flap;
Their hesitation, jerking heads, mayhap
Combine with strengthened leaves, with juice that we

Feel irritated rise, till finally
A gesture will transcend them, rounding out
And so extended—all in fine ascent

But always coldly with the dark to be
Brought down as rain new care will bring about:
How to maintain the place with best intent.

(23) Reply

The vault yet climbs above each old support,
The capitals with sharp acanthus leaves;
Yet passing time appears what chiefly grieves
The bard: it man's endeavors will abort.

A temple built will dire destruction court:
The death of cultures, of what each believes,
The passing-out-of-being that bereaves
We see in scar of storm on hardest fort.

The columns with their capitals on trees
Were modeled, likely, with nostalgia seen
For tranquil shelter of the forest green.

The statues that of soul appear to speak,
So pale and chaste, were painted by the Greek
In hues that age has drained of youthful ease.

(24) God in the Middle Ages

And within them gladly he'd been spared,
And they wanted him to be, and guide,
And, like weights, were hanging at his side
(Heav'n-ascent preventing, if he dared)

Through what their cathedrals would present:
Burden, mass. And he would merely need
To ensure his numberless be lent
Circling indications, hours to heed,

Markings on the clock for action every day.
Yet, at once, he came to function here,
And the people of the town in shock

Let him (with his voice conveying fear)
Carry on his work of striking in his way—
Fleeing from the dial of the clock.

(24) Reply

Running over rhythm, hear explode
Suddenly a stroke of wretched luck!
Olden certainties of crowning faith erode,
Swept by flood away in muck.

Even writers of the Book of Job
Couldn't pen a clear, coherent tale—
God with orb and scepter, crimson robe,
Hid, in vale of tears, behind a veil.

Schlage doch, gewünschte Stunde! wrote
Bach, a higher vision piercing through
Graveyard-gray of world to radiant-blue.

Crash! Hexameters return: the thunder smote
Earth. The wander-wind's a wailing wraith.
Making verse: my daily faith.

(25) Morgue

They lay prepared, as if intent to find
A helpful after-act to reconcile
Themselves with cold, and to each other bind.
It seemed without an ending, for awhile

A thing postponed. In someone's pocket must
A written name not next be sought, and found?
The feeling made of boredom and disgust
The cleaners of their mouths had washed around

But not away, though lips more pure may be.
The hair is stiffer on the bearded-faced
And yet made orderly, to warden's taste,

That yawner's thoughts be not too disarranged.
The eyes behind the lids are wholly changed;
They've turned around, so they within may see.

(25) Reply

Who walk through life, unsullied clarity
Undimmed within their eyes, a weightless air
Attain as of a one who here or there
Cannot remain; his mission-word: to see.

He does a daily vision-work for me:
Yet how unlike the staring Baudelaire
Who writes of corpse and carcass with a care
To shock, and even this do mockingly.

Who's Rilke? Jesus of the legend kind
Nizami told, the saint that when the crowd
About a hound-cadaver shouted loud

And proudly their revulsion and disdain,
Replied to them that, selfish, had been blind,
"The teeth are white as pearl." A jawdrop gain.

(26) The Captive

I

My hand has only one
Gesture, refusing what they foist;
And on the olden stone
The crag dropped something moist.

I hear alone this plopping
And my heart stops still
With the process of the dropping
And lacks all will.

Did the drops fall fleeter,
A beast might come to see.
Somewhere, it had been sweeter—.
But what know we?

II

Imagine what is wind now, heaven-space,
Air for your lips and brightness, eye to grace,
Was rock all 'round, ev'n to the little place
Where barely rested heart and hands and face.

And what in you is "morning" named, and "then"
And "later," maybe, and "next year," and more
Became a fester-wound that pus would pour,
Unbroken boil whose like no man will ken.

And all that was, became insane and raged
Around you, and the mouth that never laughed
Now foamed with laughter, as the man were daft.

What had been God was but the warden, ag'd,
And through the only hole whence rock was gone
Peered with a filthy eye. Yet you lived on.

(26) Reply: Alexander Pushkin's
"The Captive"

I sit behind bars in a dungeon laid bare.
An eagle, still young, brought up captive, is there.
Sad comrade, his pinions are flapping. His mood
Despondent, he pecks at his blood-covered food.

He pecks it, rejects it, is looking inside,
As if he had thought it was time we defied
Our fate, for a call are his look and his cry:
He shouts to me, "Out of here! Come, let us fly!—

We're free!—you're my comrade! Come, brother, let's
    go!
Where cloud-covered mountains are gleaming with
    snow,
Where waves of the sea flood the shore, let us roam
Wherever the winds and we birds have our home!"

(27) The Panther

in the Botanic Garden, Paris

His look has by the passing of the bars
Become so weary it can hold no more.
A seeming thousand of them, constant jars
To mind: behind them, there's no world in store.

The walk, so gentle-flexible and strong,
Small roundings making, daily littler still,
Is like a dance of power, overlong,
Around a mighty though a deafened will.

Eye-pupils' curtain will at times be viewed
In quiet raised—A picture suddenly
Will enter limbs' extended quietude
And in the heart will cease to be.

(27) Reply

(1)
Konstantin Balmont's "The Panther"

Well made and motley—laggard, hot when sated—
Three days he'll sleep—and afterward, awaking,
Will have a hounding premonition. Aching,
The call to hunt! He's growling, agitated.

The tail a-swinging, lazily he goes.
The fur is dappled, and a golden sheen
Will glimmer. Someone noted once the keen
Fine eye's a candle, that uncanny glows.

The pleasant smell of him the air can fill.
The muezzeen, on the steep of Georgian hill,
The panther hymned, who warmest love had won.

As aloe, thickly fragrant, swelled the song.
Snow-leopard singer, he had known him long—
With bloody dusk enflamed, unsettling sun.

(2)
Ella the Cat

Reclining on her back in playful style,
Near-napping, she is flirting, face half hid
Behind an auburn pillow, where are thrid
Lines white and black, together to beguile

The viewer with her brindled fur where these
Three color-friends a tapestry have made
In tufted weave—or, say, a serenade.
Hind feet part-raised in air, the shadows tease

In dialogue with darker patches. Chin
And cheeks and forepaws lit in snowy tone,
The landscape of her form has emblem grown:
Coquettish pet—sly bliss within.

(28) The Gazelle

Gazella dorcas

Enchanted, she: the best of doubled word
Can never reach the rhyming-level, higher,
That comes and goes in you, sign viewed and heard.
So from your brow will laurel rise, and lyre,

And all in you is likeness-thought aloft
In songs of love: the loving words are soft
As, to the one who reads no more, may feel
Rose-leaves on eyes that, shut, will spirit seal

To see you: borne away in spring, in leap,
Upon your course of joy, enchanted path,
Who cannot go astray if head will keep

Alert and poised to hear: as in her bath
In woods a bather, standing still in grace:
The forest lake reflected in her face.

(28) Reply

Then can we wonder why the Persians love
To give the name of *gházal* to a kind
Of writing that "gazelle" will bring to mind?
Or think of the *qasídah,* sweet as dove,

That, in Arabian elegiac style,
Begins with a nostalgic opening:
We the Beloved, just departed, sing,
Whom though we seek for many a weary mile

We shall not find: the fire, the path are gone.
Tradition will the apt apprentice tell:
The maiden to compare to a gazelle

May compensate for loss, and make less wan
The haggard loving countenance bereft,
Recapturing her tenderness from theft.

(29) The Unicorn

The holy one his head had raised: the prayer
Fell backward like a helmet from that head:
For soundless neared the never-credited
White beast that seemed as one from robber fled,
A helpless doe, entreaty-eyed in care.

The legs, more delicate than ivory,
Were moving in a symmetry of ease,
Through fur white radiance glinting sacredly;
And on the beast-brow, quiet, light, 'mid trees,
Stood, like a moonlit tow'r, horn bright to see;
His gait maintained the straight proprieties.

When lips that were with rosy gray soft-downed
Pulled back a little, you would see the white
(Supremely white); the teeth it gleaming crowned;
The nostrils raised a bit in languor light;
And yet the gaze, that nothing ever bound,
Threw images in space around,
And then, blue ballad at an end, shut tight.

(29) Reply: Valery Bryusov's "Unicorn"

Soft moss and tender turf caress my cheek.
A hundred-year-old grove. The twilight—green.
Elves flitter. Gnome will from a crevice peek.
Gaze granites. Unicorn—too briefly seen.

My spirit—why are you not free and whole?
Why flames a raging furnace in my breast?
Who destined me to flame—assumed the role
Of judge?—cold Norns have planned a cruel test!

O freedom, peace! by the familiar way
To caves where gnomes in idle spirit play—
To sing with daughters of the Forest King,

Or with the moss, the earth, the granite sleep ...
But no! a mean, unsated voice will keep
Awaking me—a clock with copper ring.

(30) Saint Sebastian

As one lying still he stands: beneath
Stern restraint maintained, of greater will.
Far, reserved, like women when they're still,
And within himself bound up: a wreath.

And the arrows come: again, again,
From his loins appearing to have sprung;
Iron, trembling-ended, there they've hung.
Yet he darkly smiles, unharmed by pain—

Sadness only once arising high,
While the eyes in dolor sore will lie;
Littleness, denying, mind will fling,
As contempt might see it falling by,
The destroyer of a lovely thing.

(30) Reply

Freedom gaining when we disregard
Our assailers' power—that is hard.
Origin of plague—the victim-loins:
Blindness you and your accuser joins.

Shelley proved Prometheus a free
Spirit. Why? Denying deity
Had the strength to chain him, he escaped—
Multitudes around him, too, reshaped.

Simple, this: Prometheus, unbound,
Knew himself and Jupiter uncrowned.
Think: Sebastian-arrows—do they hound
You as Furies did Prometheus?
Free your soul from Superego, thus
Uninfuriated freeing us.

(31) The Donor

It was commissioned by the painters' guild.
The Savior he had, maybe, never seen;
Nor holy Bishop, with demeanor stilled,
Was ever by his side, as here was willed,
Nor laid a hand upon him, calm, serene.

Perhaps the point was merely *thus* to kneel
(The point of what we, too, well understand):
To kneel—one's contours each contained to feel,
Transcendence-wanting, altogether spanned,
Held in the heart, as horses by the hand,

So, if a thing enormous would take place—
Undocumented and unprophesied—
We'd hope that, keeping well away its face,
It nearer came, quite near, within our space,
In self-concern, self-deepened, to abide.

(31) Reply

That god should not directly gaze at me
Would surely be the best, I'm well advised:
What bale awaited eager Semele
Whom Hera plagued with seed of doubt, that she
Might want to see her lover undisguised!

He neared—alas! that such a thing should be!—
Whom when she viewed afar, she realized,
Though dimly yet, her grand calamity
And trembled as a leaf on aspen tree
In fear of soon beholding what she'd prized.

Now nearer, nearer seen!—that brilliancy
Whereof no prophet eye could have apprised
The suppliant, who prayed on bended knee
She'd not be burned—vain yearning not to see
Her Zeus!—consuming flame she'd not surmised.

(32) The Angel

He with a nodding of his brow unbound
And scattered what constrained and what confined;
For through his heart's uprising to the mind
The Ever-coming, whirling 'round.

The heaven-deeps are filled with figures, and
Each one will summon him: Come, recognize—
Your hands keep light in leaving all that tries
To burden. They'd have come—they'd understand—

By night, yet harsher struggle-test to show,
And rampaged through the house in might of ire,
And, as if they had made you, seized you, so
They from your form might break you forth entire.

(32) Reply

O Lord! an angel is a terror: save
To him who, Spirit-true, would loving win
The glory forced by Gabriel! Within
The narrow breast a soul-enfolding cave

Was opened when a heart was purified
By three that like the Abram-angels came
On errand strange, that speck of Adam-blame
The Indefectible might set aside.

With high desire that can withstand the jinn,
The burdened earth is gravid, and the grave,
That ancient gate, is adoration-door:

The fire can rise that, clay-encased before,
Will now with shine defy the Satan-shame
And look on Heaven brave and angel-eyed.

(33) Roman Sarcophagus

Why should we not believe, or speculate
(Though here we all are scattered, disarranged)
Not brief's the time that only pressure, hate,
And muddle stayed in us, today unchanged,

As once in the sarcophagal display
With combat, god-form, goblet, ribbon—all
'Mid slow-consumed old fabrics' draping fall—
A slowly-loosened something lay—

Till unknown mouths had swallowed it at last,
That never speak. (And is there any brain
Yet thinking that to these, the silent, goes?)

By aqueducts throughout our human past
Eternal waters fresh-conducted came—:
In them it yet is mirrored, shines, and flows.

(33) Reply

The shining and the mirroring are bright,
The pressure, hate, and muddle rather dark.
The loosening is double: loose and light
Are easy morals—yet a vital spark

May be from welcome disentangling freed.
What is the Roman riddle, do you think?
It seems a thing whereby we climb and sink:
Perhaps the freedom of a human deed.

For Adam's liberty full soon would prove
The enigmatic fruit we must digest;
The Discord Apple caused the Trojan war.

So what are brothers always fighting for?
Of animals are we the worst and best.
The thirst to be the first—old apple core.

(34) The Swan

Tiredness, heavily proceeding on,
Through the not-yet-done, and as if bound:
Uncreated movement of the swan.

Death, a no-more-doing of the ground—
That which we must daily stand upon—
Of his fearful self-allowing-down—:

Into waters, that him gently had,
And that, as if vanished, as if glad,
Backward, flood on flood, can move below;
While, unending-quiet and secure,
Yet more royal, ever worldlier,
So relaxed, they let him rest and flow.

(34) Reply

Here a metamorphing has been made,
Death transmuted to a more-than-calm,
Swan of Tuonela new-portrayed.

Cool and shady river overlaid
With a motion, for the soul a balm,
Of a swan who wanders unafraid.

Not a Styx, nor yet a Phlegethon,
Nothing here of age and woe and pain,
Joy denial of an Acheron.
He'll abandonment and freedom gain

Who Islamic Eden may have found:
Ample rivers rolling underground.

(35) Childhood

It would be good to think a bit if we
Would something say of what is lost and gone:
Long childhood afternoons that, moving on,
Came never back. A riddle, we agree.

We're warned—perchance it happens during rain—
But we no longer know what lies in store;
Our lives would never be so full again
Of meeting, re-encounter, wand'ring more,

As then, when nothing happened save the way
It happens to a thing or to a beast:
We lived our humanness as they, at least,
And to the brim were filled with figure-play,

And shepherd-like became in solitude,
And distance-overladen in the head,
And summoned as from far, and touched in mood,
And slow, as if by thread, prolonged, renewed,
To sequences of pictures we'd be led,
Where now we stay, with bafflement imbued.

(35) Reply

for Sarah

He who binds to himself a joy
Does the winged life destroy
But he who kisses the joy as it flies
Lives in eternity's sun rise.
                    —*William Blake, "Eternity"*

I think of childhood as the time
When little's meant by such a rhyme:
Long sunny summer afternoon;
And easy rain and thunder soon.

To swing in shady playground fair,
Held deftly in the rhythmed air,
Had meant we felt the season move
In gentle wind, in swaying love.

Columbus' famed discovery
Would pale when Sarah said one day,
"Dad, I'm a me, and you're a me;
We're all—we're me's!" What more to say?

She further, at the age of five,
When morning dawns are fire-alive,
Would startlingly one day deplore
The way things finer were at four.

Sublime the findings: marvels all,
Unhardened into rise or fall
When willfulness won't bind our joys,
And wingéd life no pride destroys.

(36) The Poet

You hour, you're moving away from me.
Your wingbeat wounds when it moves away.
But what to do with my mouth—you see?
And with my night? and with my day?

I've no beloved, no home, no plea,
No place to live in, or where to stay.
The things I give myself to—they
Get rich, and they distribute me.

(36) Reply

Time isn't gone, a present yet,
And when I feel depletion, drained,
By silent emptihead beset
As of a robin reft and pained,

The fledged I follow while I let
Them fly. Their faces have remained:
I dreaming eye what I have gained—
And find in air the lines have met.

(37) The Lace

I

Mankind: a wavering possession's name,
Of luck an even weaker element:
Is it inhuman that the lace would claim—
This little, thick, close-woven present lent—
Two human eyes? You want them back? You blame?

You, long departed now and lastly blind,
Is your beatitude within this thing
In which, as 'tween the trunk and bark to cling,
Your feeling, altered, shrunk, might pleasure find?

Slipped through a little gap, a crack in fate,
Your spirit from your era you withdrew,
And so this open, light-filled thing will state,
And make me smile, the usefulness to view.

II

And if some day we may begin to muse:
These facts, and what is happening with us
Are trivial, too strange, too frivolous
To make it worth outgrowing baby shoes
Indeed, for this—or merely think: the way
Of yellowed lace with densely twined device,
That lacy flowered road—would it suffice
To hold us here? But look: they're *done*, they stay.

A life perhaps had been despised, who knows?
Some gladness here and there had been surrendered,
And in the end, whatever profit grows,
This thing, not lighter than the life, was tendered
And finished, and so fine as might afford
Right time to smile, to float with those adored.

(37) Reply

Hand-illustrated folded candle screen;
The "token" album: sketches, paper scraps ...
On glass, wood, china, ribbon, ivory,
Or velvet it was "fancy work" to paint.

Chinoiserie in pen-work gaily seen
On jewel-box, tea-caddy; or perhaps
You'd faux-bamboo a chair (draw carefully!),
Or: bristle-brushed, sieve-spattered, free of taint,

A densely patterned stencil would adorn
A blanket, lamp or quilt, or wicker chair;
With scissors and a pot of gum appear
A gold-framed linen-paper filigree;

On greeting cards we also like to see
A silhouette; and floral cutouts born
Of myriad pinpricks for the petals clear;
Collage of colored papers rich and rare.

These cover less than half the handcraft book
Of *Period Pastimes* gathered by Felice
Hodges to show the range of lady-art:
Four hundred years summed up, to please the eye.

The will to decoration well may look
As if a sentence granting no release
Were uttered by a judge; and yet the heart
Is touched; frail things we make, and then we die.

(38) A Woman's Fate

Much as a king who's on a hunt might seize
A glass to drink from, give it little thought,
And then the one who had it, keeps it; he's
Put it away, forgotten like as not:

So maybe Fate at times would, thirstily
As well, a cup fortuitously raise,
Then, fearing lest the life be broken, She
Would keep it, quite unused, for many days,

In glazen case with fragile items, where
The valuable objects were maintained
(Or things for which a value might be claimed)—

Long, like an alien thing, remaining there,
And merely growing old, becoming blind,
No longer valued now, and not deemed rare.

(38) Reply: Igor Severyanin's "Sonnet"

The landscape of her face, in finer, lively way
With lover-bodies in vibration, mind in spring,
High-spirited in beauty, made me wish, that day,
I might imprint it for a future marveling.

The fragrant silk of flaxen locks a lunar gleam
No artist render may in watercolors rare.
Her gaze alone that glimmered in a languid dream
With twofold anguish had appeared to glisten there.

How strange I felt before that portrait—ill and
    pained—
Such pain as in the longest while I'd never known.
And it appeared to me within that study, drained

Of all but desperation, hard rebukes had grown.
She looked toward the window. Myriads of years
Would I be doomed to wander in a land of tears.

(39) A Woman Recovering

As a lane-brought song will come and go,
Near to draw, and then to shy away,
Wing aflap, as we might catch it so,
Then, in farther streaming on, to stray,

Life with one recovering will play,
Who, while gently resting, weariedly,
Helpless, in a meek surrender, may
Shape a gesture that we rarely see.

She will come to feel as if seduced
When her rough and hardened hand, wherein
Fevers had arisen, late unloosed,
May from far with blooming touch begin
Gently to caress her roughened chin.

(39) Reply

Why think it a seduction to relax?
Our mind and heart we over-, under-tax.
A man abandoned by his wife explained
To me how he some freedom had regained:

He thought abandonment a tragedy
Although he'd not been married happily.
He talked of it with a psychologist
And told of that Beloved whom he missed ...

When speaking of the marriage, he'd admit
That there were benefits to ending it—
Yet melancholy ruled. What must he do?
"Have you been governed by the thought that you
Could do no better?" Maybe *there*'s a clue ...

(40) The Grown-up Woman

It all stood up before her. World it was,
And stood right up before her, fear and grace,
A standing tree to grow by granted laws,
All image, imageless, a Holy Ark
As on a people placed, and solemn-dark.

And she would bear it, bore it up, away—
The flying, fleeing, and the farther-turned,
The vast, enormous, never fully learned—
Relaxed as one who's bearing, shall we say,
Filled water jug. Till 'mid the playful spell,
Preparing, altered, something more beside,
The first white veil with gentle, airy glide
Over the open countenance then fell

Translucent, barely, and no more to rise
And to her questions somehow vague replies
Would offer, only, while she strained to view:
In you, you child-that-was, in you, in you.

(40) Reply

If we no longer as a child can see
With livened mind the wonder of our being,
It is the languor of our apathy,
The film of our familiarity,
That, dulling cataract, will stop our seeing.

So Coleridge told, and later Shelley said
The same in the defense of poetry
He wrote to show extended empathy
A hampered heart to legislation led
Whereby the Law of Love would come to be.

But childhood had to Wordsworth taught that we
When in a vacant or a pensive mood
Through wealth of gazing could be rich as he
And child-self might revive, with pow'r endued
Of inward eye, the bliss of solitude.

(41) Tanagra

A little bit of well-tanned earth,
As if it were by sun-heat burned:
As if the gesture came to birth
In hand of girl at last returned,
Recovered, never lost again;
With nothing left of longing then
For anything not here within
That, from her feeling, out might lead,
But touching only self indeed,
As when a hand might stroke a chin.

We bring it up; we draw
A figure, and one more;
We cannot grasp the law
Whereby it stayed, we saw;
We only ought to pore
More deeply, wonder-filled,
On former being, or
To smile: more clear-instilled
Than 'twas the year before.

(41) Reply

A spot of time brought back
That we had thought to lack;
A feeling we had known,
To part of mind now grown—
That, granted memory,
Will not recanted be;
The gift of past to self
As of domestic elf;
A calmness that the brain
In tranquil alms will gain.

Traverse Tanagra in your dream:
Attentive be to what may seem
A patch of light where one might drown
When mantra-chanting, glancing down.
The ground, like ancient figurine
That in Hellenic town was made,
New-favored by the sun, will mean
The gold-alembicated scene
May wealth of mental gain unlade.

(42) The Dazzling Woman

She sat, much as the others did, at tea.
I thought at first, though, that perhaps the way
She held her cup had differed, so to say.
Her laughter, once—it hit me painfully.

And when they finally arose and talked
And slowly, as by chance it would occur
(While speaking, laughing), through the rooms they
    walked
And then she followed them, I looked at her:

Held back she seemed, as one who suddenly
Would be obliged to sing—for many, too;
Upon her happy eye, so bright to view,
As on a pond, an outdoor ray I'd see.

She followed slowly and required delay
As if some obstacle she must get by
And, having traveled past her passageway,
She'd glad abandon walking and would fly.

(42) Reply: Alexander Pushkin's "Poet"

Until Apollo calls the bard
Unto the holy sacrifice,
In this vain world he'll find it hard
To throw off all that would entice.
The sacred lyre as yet is quiet.
In dreamy stupefaction he
Was drawn to worldliness, and by it
Attracted, sank to nullity.

    No sooner does the godly word,
However, touch his eager ear
Than, like an eagle startled, stirred,
The poet knows the time is near.
His spirit boredom no more bridles,
He flees the gossip of the crowd—
Before the feet of others' idols
That noble forehead no more bowed.
Severe and wild, he'll run, he'll rove,
Possessed by tones that rush and rave,
Toward the shore, the wailing wave,
To the reverberating grove ...

(43) In a Foreign Park

Borgeby-Gård

There are two ways. And neither leads away.
But one, at times, in thought, will yet allow
A farther passage. Seems you went astray,
Then rounded flower beds before you lay;
Alone are you with single gravestone now:
Of British Baroness Sophia say
The name and date; the traces in decay
You with your finger feel; the fading year—
Why don't they even less to you appear?

Why do you waver, as at first when you
Expectant came this court of elms to view,
That's damp and dark and never walked upon?

What kind of contradiction leads you on
To seek, as if it were a rose's name,
What you might find on sunny bloom-bed lit?

Why stand so often still? What do you hear?
Why moths uncover, finally, that came
Bewildered, on the high-grown phlox to flit?

(43) Reply

Hard won, the confidence required to write
A lyric answerless and question-laden.
I'll follow that example and will pose
The query why in quiet I enclose
Myself as death embraced the quiet maiden,
And, like a butterfly, attractive light
To focus on, prefer the tranquil dark
And, nearly tone-bereft, the muffled stream
The quiet ear is lent, as in the park

The stranger felt encompassed by a dream
Of roundness unevadable, the elms
Embracing flower beds. The moths, the phlox

All stopping short of symbol. Overwhelms
The reader the enigma while it mocks
The questioner with emblem-lexicon.

I'm minded, oddly, of Henri Rousseau:
By sleeping tiger, giant palm we go
Into a primitivity long gone.

(44) Parting

How I have felt what parting pow'r can mean!—
And know it still: a dark not overcome,
A dreadful thing, bound loveliness wherefrom
Restraint appears and rends apart unseen.

What weakness did it leave!—to need to see
What, when it called, appeared to let me go—
But stayed, as if there had remained with me
Women, so white, so little—nothing, though,

But this: a nod, yet not to me, now shown—
A softly-leading-on, with riddling air,
Explainable no more: a plum-tree fair,
Perhaps, from which a cuckoo, quick, had flown.

(44) Reply: Comment on Emily Dickinson's "Parting"

My life closed twice before its close—
It yet remains to see
If Immortality unveil
A third event to me,

So huge, so hopeless to conceive,
As these that twice befell.
Parting is all we know of heaven,
And all we need of hell.

How varied will the parting be:
The cuckoo mocks the plum;
Bereavement fells more rendingly
Emily Dickinson.

Hell-empty heaven-fantasy—
But one departure-story:
We tell some more, and then we see
Levels of purgatory.

(45) Experiencing Death

We nothing of the end-surrender know
That nothing shares with us. No ground have we
Admiring love or hounding enmity
To death, with his distorting mask, to show—

A mask-mouth, to a dirge inclined with ease.
The world is filled with roles we have to play.
So long as we're concerned *to please,* I say,
Death plays along, though *he* may never please.

But when you went, onto the stage there burst
A strip of the reality that could
Come through the split through which you left, the
      first
Gleam of real green, real sunshine, and real wood.

We're playing on. What fear and effort taught
You say, and make a gesture now and then;
Your odd, turned-backward being, far from men,
Can overcome us, 'mid this play we've wrought,

At times, as if 'twere knowledge of the laws
Of the reality that sinks away,
So we, a moment rent afar, can play
At life awhile, not thinking of applause.

(45) Reply

Gleams in the irises of eyes,
Shine on the skins of writhing fish:
Weird intermingled fear and wish!
Bewilder-images arise

When we imagine what we love:
Light of desired approval. My
Face, in parental mirror-eye,
Beams kindly from a height above.

Yet glitter-fish Orestes found
In Jeffers' lyric: shedding foam,
Jostled, abducted from their home,
Mutual bitter mirrors, bound

And compassed in a cruel net.
So us, reflection by our friends,
The will to please them, deathward bends,
Our tarnished silver shining yet.

The need to please, the need to please,
A trouble to the muddled young,
Adults may lend a serpent tongue,
Dead-spirit-turned in seeming ease.

(46) Blue Hydrangea

Last green in pots where colors melded are,
These leaves appear, how muted, raw, and dry,
Behind the umbels that no blue of sky
Now bear, but only mirror from afar.

They mirror vaguely, who have had their cry,
As if they'd gladly lose it all again,
As with old, faded letter-papers when
Their violet, gray, yellow meet the eye.

Outgrown—so like a children's pinafore
That nothing happens to—it's worn no more:
A little life—we feel the brevity.

But blue—it seems renewing instantly:
In but a single umbel one can see
The touching blue a joy in green outpour.

(46) Reply

Sweet tea hydrangeal is in Japan
Served to the ones who come to celebrate
The Buddha's birthday feast on April 8.
They first upon the statue of the man

Pour down the *ama-cha,* as dragons poured
Amrita (drink *amortal*, deathless) when
The one who taught the doctrine best to men
Appeared who was to be the demons' lord.

So blue—the soul-refreshing hue of sky,
Which when we look upon we're lifted high
Ev'n as the tree can make the viewer tall.

How blue the roof in heaven's father-hall,
Who had a favored son, and you are he!
Let blest Kwan-Yin your heaven-mother be.

(47) Before the Summer Rain

At once, from all that's green within the park
One knows not what, a something, overcome,
Taken, one feels him near the window, dumb.
Only insistently, and strong and stark,

A running sound above through eave-trough
        streams:
I think of loneliness, and of Jerome,
The solitary scholar—zeal of dreams,
All from that tone—who roaring pour and foam

Would hear. The taller ballroom walls appear
With all their pictures now to have withdrawn
As if they heard no longer what we say.

The trodden carpets mirror, color gone,
The dim uncertain light of later day
When as a child one felt a nearing fear.

(47) Reply

A hint apocalyptic made the light
Flicker as if El Greco felt the gleam.
A saint in rocky cleft or cave would seem
To hear a something that evaded sight.

A child, or animal, the graying stirs,
Flashing in eyes that, widened, prophesy
The coming rumble in the wind that whirrs
And what will crash, and shake the walls—and why?

No one had pointed out, when I was young,
That there were those who could divide the mind
So that the wakeful brain, its feeling-part,

Would fear the lightning and the making-blind;
That, having sealed their impress on the heart,
These might be spoken by the poet-tongue.

(48) In the Reception Room

I find the men surrounding us, who go
In fancy-dress of chamberlain, jabots,
Are getting slowly darker like the night
Around their order-stars' high-handed light;
The ladies, tender, fragile, dressed to seem
More bulky—little hand in lap will gleam
Slim as a ribbon for a Bolognese—
Surrounding all: the reader, if you please,
And the observer of each bibelot:
And most of these they own, I think you know.

With perfect tact, they leave us speaking so,
To lead our life as we conceive it, and
As they our days will never understand.
They want to bloom, be beautiful—and we
Would ripen, darkly strive, yet do, not be.

(48) Reply

You know them by their fruit, not bloom,
Who gather so in heaven-room
That rondure of the Being we
Conceive which can the mind illume.

A darkness in the heart will be
The garden plot where seedlings free,
From out the night that flame encased,
The germinating jujube tree.

The dark, the night had one embraced
Who in the quiet brave had faced
The agüe of the marrow bone,
For warm the blood in flood had raced.

From the alone to the Alone
We go, but when the stars have thrown
Their farthest fire to heat the gloom,
Let our *amen* outshout the moan.

(49) Last Evening

from the collection of Frau Nonna

And night, and farther faring; troops on board,
The train was quickly moving past the park.
His gaze he lifted from the clavichord,
Kept playing, and would look at her, and hark,

For she had like a mirror to him grown:
Filled with his features, youthful all the more,
And seeming as if all his grief she bore,
Lovelier, more seductive with each tone.

But suddenly it all seemed wiped away:
She in the window niche with effort stood
And stilled her beating urgent heart instead.

His playing ceased. Fresh air, from far away.
So alien lay upon the table-wood
The shako, black, adorned by headbone dead.

(49) Reply

I see the nightmare hat upon a desk
In dreams of warhead leaders, army hat
With centered head of death. Too Kafkaesque?
You ask. I answer: how *banal* is that?

A "war on terror" is a war without
An enemy. Abstraction can you kill?
Wage Peace Today requires a different will.
Our madness flaunting, sanity we flout.

Our fighters are committing suicide.
They flee the grisly crimes they cannot hide.
The shako with the skull had shaken them.

Awake! Unless the rule of death we stem,
We'll nothing prove, but spread the realm of hate,
The skeleton be helmsman of the state.

(50) Picture of My Father in His Youth

In eye, a dream. The forehead touched, beguiled
By something distant. 'Round the mouth a vast
Amount of youth, allurement yet unsmiled.
Before the uniform, tight, slender-styled,
Both noble and complete, in fashion past,
The saber cord, and quiet, resting hands
That tranquil wait, that naught to act would bind,
Yet nearly seen no longer, as if these—
That tried to grasp the future—none can find.
All intimately with itself entwined,
And yet dissolved, as if none understands;
And deep, from its own depth, with dull unease—

Daguerreotype, you're vision swift that flees
My fleeting hands that hold you—unconfined …

(50) Reply

I came like water, and like wind I go,
The Persian poet stoically said.
But we, to speed them up, our blood let flow
That tulips, new, no longer slowly grow
But be with carmine ardor quickly fed.
A friend a photo yesterday had mailed
Who said that if two soldiers, young and old,
The latter's head on former's breast, had failed
To move the viewing mind to comprehend
How youth and age are equally in bold
Devotion well combined and lesson lend
Of what we honor, visiting their tombs—

O anguish amorous! In these there looms
Unwise, untimely, frightening, the end.

(51) Self-Portrait from the Year 1906

Of long and old aristocratic line
A trace remains in eyebrow-structure fine.
His look maintains a childhood's fear and hue
And here and there a meekness, not of true
Servant, but one who serves, and womanly;
The mouth a proper mouth, distinct to see,
Not overspeaking, only what is right
To utter. And the forehead blemish-free
Fit for the shade of quiet looking down.

A unity intuited through sight;
Yet not in sorrow, neither in success
Gathered in lasting penetratingness,
But as, made up of scattered things around,
Afar were planned an earnest work of might.

(51) Reply: Self-Portrait from the Year 1969

Desiring, solitary, to be liked,
He yet, to merit such a liking, is
Convinced a high design to serve will his
Requirement be, for teacher-life well psyched.
He can't be happy till he finds a way
To blend the strict performance of a duty
With votive labor for diviner beauty.
He'll study revelation-lore that may
Unveil new sky and earth, new night and day.

Until he has retired, he'll waste a great
Amount of time and thought (an office clerk!)
In student essay-draft correction work.
He'll flame in sudden waking when he's old.
At least, at last, the hidden goal is told.

(52) The King

The King is but sixteen years of age,
Sixteen years, and already the State.
He looks, as from ambush, reserved and sage,
Past graybeard chamberlains great—

Just randomly rounding the hall, within,
And nothing feels but these:
On the narrow, long, and hardened chin,
The coldened hairs of the fleece.

The death decree his eye invites,
The space for name long blank.
They think: how he hesitates.

They know him so well, they think (and thank):
He'll be the kind that till seventy waits
Before his name he writes.

(52) Reply

Self-portrait! We know it at once!
Young, you think? But already prepared
(Though huckster and hustler may call him dunce),
He can wait awhile: he dared.

It's nice to be young, when the years remain
An invitation—when, undeterred,
Determined, interminables attain
The ones with the waiting word.

I rise in the morning and note:
The psychopomp came and went.
But he left me the key of the legend gate.

O maker of gold I devote
My day to explaining the lesson lent:
I'll write. I've learned to wait.

(53) Resurrection

The count hears tones that quake;
He sees a rent of light;
His thirteen sons he'll wake
From burial-night.

He greets his wives, the both;
Respectful, distant he.
All trustful, nothing loth,
They rise to eternity

And wait for Eric, unseen,
And Ulrica Dorothy;
At seven and thirteen

(In sixteen-ten, must be)
They died on Flanders field,
And so today we yield

To them priority.

(53) Reply

I'd days unconscious lain
And mumbled, rarely, slow.
My mother came: to her pain,
I shouted: she must *go!*

They told me I'd lost an ear;
All right, I'd yet the one.
Some watercolors clear
They lent me; pure, and fun.

And a silken bed-robe, too,
My aunt had sent by air.
Each robe- and painter-hue

So fine in childhood flair,
I thought, while dreams I drew:
I am but twenty-one.

My life has re-begun.

(54) The Standard Bearer

The others feel: all's raw about them there,
Off-putting: iron, leather, and that gear.
At times a flatt'ring feather may appear,
But each is lonely, loveless, no one dear;
Yet he alone—as if a wife he'd bear—
The ensign keeps in festal covering:

Thick-wrapped behind him, heavy silken thing,
That up above his hands at times will fly.

He can alone, if he will shut his eye,
A smile perceive: he won't abandon her.

When come with cuirasses in lightning-whirr
The ones who struggle and to seize her try,

Then from the staff he's bound to tear her down,
As if she had from maidenhead been rent—
Thus, under weapon-cover, safety lent:—

That's, for the others, courage, fame, his crown.

(54) Reply

Reproaches none, but only empathy:
No love abandon, ye that enter in.
Though death surround, he's found a thing to win
His willing heart, though killing be a sin;
For love is what we are, and if it be
Denied it will emerge in altered form.

O ensign, angel in a shape enorm!
The banner and the oriflamme that fly

And war and carnage gladly glorify!
The fabric as the grass will wither, fade,

But comfort give, as we our woes unlade
And in our narrow home prepare to lie.

Of years how few, how full of trouble, we!
Whose glory is a halo 'round a cloud,
Whereunder we are blinded, bent, and bowed,

Returned to earth, new-termed eternity.

(55) The Last Count of Brederode
Evades Capture by the Turks

They followed, horrible, and motley-hued
Death-menace casting after him, while he
Forlorn would run, though not past threat pursued.
The distance of his fathers seemed to be

No longer of importance: thus to flee
Will any beast from hunter. Lightning-vision:
Uprushed the water near! And One Decision
Uplifted him and all his woe; you see

Him servant, once again, of princely line.
Aristocratic ladies' smile would feed
Once more with sweet his newly young and fine

Completed countenance. He spurred the steed
(Large blood-brimmed heart of both!) to flood and
        foam:
It bore him, as to castle heading home.

(55) Reply

Some face the flood with aid of maid adored;
Some pray for succor from their holy lord;
For others yet a battle flag may be
The guardian of grace, to watch and ward.

Enthusiasm, Adam-youthful, poured
As fruitful wine of striving soul-accord,
Empowering the pilgrim, soon will he
For Promised Land the River Jordan ford.

As life is brief, we'll be requiring speed.
The playfulness of racing will indeed
Instill, fulfill the move-inducement need.

Let rivals in Olympic lines compete:
No comrade grudges wreath to one more fleet;
If love is judge, there cannot be defeat.

(56) The Courtesan

The sun of Venice will within my hair
The gold, as noble outcome, now prepare
Of alchemy. And, too, the eyebrows fair
May be to bridges likened: look how they

Above the hidden dangers lead away
Of eyes, that a secreted traffic lead
Along canals, and make the seas indeed
Arise in them and fall and alter. He'd

Be jealous of my dog—the man who'd see
How often during a distracted rest,
The hand that by no heat was ever charred,

Unwoundable, adorned, would tenderly
Enclasp it. Hopes of ancient line, the best,
When touched by venomed mouth of mine, are
        marred.

(56) Reply

The fatal Venice-tempters we have known
From Shakespeare and from Thomas Mann are
    shown
Once more, imbued with noisome poison, grown
From deadly seed to carnal knowledge tree.

Lord Byron (*Beppo*) saw it differently.
"Just like a coffin, clasped in a canoe,
Where none can make out what you say or do"—
That's how a góndola he'd archly view.

And Goethe—witty *Epigrams of Venice*!
Priapus had escaped, and none the worse
The poet felt, on his Italian travels.

Ah no, we never get a threat, a menace—
He comes, appetitive, with furnished purse,
And Northern web and mental knot unravels.

(57) The Orangerie Stairway

Versailles

As kings, who with the habit are endued
Of striding aimlessly, and thus appear
To kneelers on the sides, in solitude
Of royal mantle on occasion, near,

So 'twixt the balustrades, that have inclined
For ages immemorial, will rise
The stairway, slow, its godly grace divined,
High heavenward though nowhere, to our eyes,

As if a step would followers below
Command to stay—that they might never dare
So high from distant lowly state to go:
The heavy royal train not one may bear.

(57) Reply

A place for everyone, and everyone
In place. And spend your days in competition
For trinkets that will parody ambition.
The King may smile: in him the State, the Sun.

The bourgeois but a figure is of fun.
Molière, with unexampled ebullition,
Disdainfully conveys him to perdition,
A tale of hapless blunder having spun.

We're courtly fools until the hour is done
When disempowered we've attained our mission:
Outshining, by a mite, our opposition,
We'll die of pride, belike, that portly gun.

(58) The Marble Transport Wagons

Paris

Divided, for the horses, seven ways,
The never-moved-before their tread allowed;
For what in midst of marble had been proud
In age, resistance, and the All, yet stays,

Beheld among the people: not unknown,
See, by who knows what name that we might say;
No—but like pressing action in a play—
Now viewed, then by the hero overthrown:

So rolls it through the stagnant course of day,
Comes on with circumstance of heavy state,
As if the Triumphator neared, the Great,

Slowly at last; before him, closer, slow,
Must captive, loaded with his burden, go.
It nears, impeding all with its delay.

(58) Reply

Of legacy outworn the deadly weight
Of which the movement is a killing halt
The memory, by monumental fault,
Must bear in torment that will not abate.

The Imperátor whom the slavish hate,
Who savorless the days of mining salt
Has made as god of elephántine vault,
Exalted mausoleum of the great,

Might even be prepared to slay his son,
As Peter had to weak Alexis done.
O dreary adulation of the State

Where empty greed's held up as holy Fate!—
Each piece of dusty gold become a gun,
Each golden heart a fated leaden weight.

(59) Buddha

The foreign far-arriving pilgrim, shy,
Already felt as if a goldenness
As of a droplet fell, as if heaped high
Were secrets that regretful realms confess.

But he became bewildered, coming near,
Before the eyebrows towering in height;
Of well-known drinking vessel naught was here,
Or pendant earring-shine, the wives' delight.

It splendid would have been if one could say
What things together had been molten, so
This form on such a flower-cup this way

Could have been set: more yellow, mute, and still
Than something made of gold—yet 'round would go
And touch one's self and, too, the room would fill.

(59) Reply

What stranger than a brave tranquillity?
More rich than silver, distant as the dawn
From busy day, where think and act, not be,
Are burden-words we bear, and carry on.

We view the men of rue, as, at his feet,
The narratives that rule the human brain
They place, and in that deed are cleansed, complete,
Freed of their boring demon-story pain.

"Unconscious"? But another name for soul,
A seër claimed—yet one they cannot save
Who must, old mimic-scriptings mulling, rave,

Imprisoned in misprision, wordy web,
And feel the tide that is our life-blood ebb:
How wide the step that led from *gaol* to *goal*!

(60) Roman Fountain

Borghese

Two basins: one above the other soaring
From out a marble round, its overflow
Of water to the neighbor softly pouring,
To water standing, waiting down below,

That to the gentle babbler's quiet, hiding
And showing, as within a hollow hand,
Behind dark greenery the sky abiding,
As if unknown and hard to understand;

Itself in chalice quiet, unrepining,
To spread, not homesick, ripples round on round,
But sometimes dreamily and droplet-crowned

Inclining to the slope where mosses grow,
As final mirror in a chalice found,
Still flowing over now, and smiling so.

(60) Reply: Conrad Ferdinand Meyer's "Roman Fountain"

The ray will rise, then falling pour
And fill the marble basin round
That veiled in turn is flowing more
To reach a lower chalice-ground;
The second lends the third below
Another flood, the wealthiest,
And each will take and lending flow
And stream and rest.

(61) The Carousel

Jardin du Luxembourg

Well-sheltered, shadow-making, turns around
A little while the carousel at hand
With colored horses hailing from the land
That waits and wavers, then no more is found.
The steeds at times may hitched to wagons be,
And all equipped with heartened mood of ease;
An angry carmine lion goes with these;
From time to time White Elephant we see.

A stag is there, as on the forest ground,
But he a saddle bears, and there espied
A small blue girl with belt is buckled 'round.

And on the lion white a youth will ride
And hold him; heated little hand has he.
The teeth and lion tongue will never hide.

From time to time White Elephant we see.

And on their horses they are sweeping past,
The girls included, bright, who leaping steed
Have pretty near outgrown; with swinging speed
Up, down they look, and straight ahead at last—

From time to time White Elephant we see.

They whirl around and hurry till the end,
They circle and they turn without an aim.
A red, a green, a gray, they gleaming send;
An outline gone before you find the name;
At times a little smile you'd like to claim,
A blissful dazzle, spent upon the game
That breathless blind duration may extend.

(61) Reply

Ineffably I love the carousel.
We've six of them, right here in Triple Cities.
I'll reminisce tonight, and little ditties
Indite, of childhood wonder thus to tell
In fantasy, than Thurber's Walter Mitty's
More overflowing with a manic spell.
Historic, they were made by Allan Herschell;
And George F. Johnson, hero of commercial

And philanthropic charity as well,
Presented them as gifts, with the condition
That they be free to children. Ring the bell!

I cannot well contain my ebullition
For Johnson and his fond, non-controversial
Fulfillment of a lifetime giving-mission,
Nor memories of child-excitement quell,

An early world in carefree light arrayed.
I used to bring my daughter; we'd go riding,
On rising horse or falling, mind be gliding
Along with the calliope that played.

I loved the up-and-down-plus-rounding motion.
I felt transported more than she, I tell you!
In happy trance, enchanting, rapt devotion,
The music and the movement would impel you:
I liked to think of boats upon the ocean,
The air itself a more-than-potent potion:
Oh, what a spell of melody befell you!

(62) The Spanish Dancing Girl

As in the hand the sulphur match of white,
Prior to flame arising, every way
Will stretch out tongues of fire, a circle bright
Of new observers see the heated light
Of widened rounding dance in twitching play.

Now: flame, and nothing more! Behold it there.

With but a glance will she enkindle hair
And spin with daring, artful, suddenly,
Her garment, all, in ardent ecstasy;
From her, like serpents that in terror rise,
Bare arms, with clicking, liven ears and eyes.

And then: as though of fire she'd had enough,
She gathers it and throws it, gesture rough,
Commanding; with the pride of what to birth
Has come, she views it raging on the earth,
The flame unyielding still in lowly place—.

But sure, triumphant, and with what a sweet
And greeting smile! she's lifting up her face
And firmly stamps it out with little feet.

(62) Reply

A film, *Flamenco,* we had come to see
Where never would we hear a spoken word
Included. Let but gesture, singing be!
So hoarse and worn the vocal tones that we
The like of them before had never heard—

And wild, impassioned with a bitter bliss.

My daughter had a theory for this:
Not only ardor throats had plundered so,
But smoking-decades made the trouble grow.
Their fervor made it plain, however: fate
Will make me prove the limits of my state.

The drama was but virtual: no plot,
No situation even. That was not
An obstacle to knowledge. In the eye
The heaven was the hell of nether sky.
The clouds were hungry, swagging on the deep,
Each arabesque of robe a whale-road wave
That moonlight would with furor-lightning lave:

Then let us rage before the reign of sleep.

(63) The Tower

Tour St.-Nicolas, Tournes

Earth-innards. And as if the thing you sought,
In blindness climbing, earthen surface were,
To which you rise from streambed steep, where stir
The brooks had made to swell, a flowing brought

By darkness; and through this today your face,
As if 'twere resurrected, you impel:
You seem to *see* that dark, as if it fell
From out this pit, its overhanging place

Above you, as it, giant, tumbling sheer,
Down rumbles in the dusk of quiet pews;
You know it, with a fear you cannot lose:
If it should rise, bedecked as 'twere a steer—:

But now you're taken from the narrow ending
By winding light, near-flying, glimpsing here
The heaven, brilliant rays that dazzle, blending,
And there the deeps, awake, alertly tending,

Each little dayscape as in Patenir,
Hours simultaneous and side-by-side,
With leaping bridges, doglike, eager-eyed,
That track the path of shining, bright and clear,

Which helpless houses may at times yet hide,
Until it in the background will subside,
And rested go through landscape-thicket wide.

(63) Reply

The purpose here appears bewilderment:
Ascending through the tower, up and down
We find reversed: the pit will switch with crown.
There is a big direction-question sent.

We too will be confused: the heaven-tent,
Where pow'rs may dwell that, light or dark, might
    frown
Or smile, and like a giant or a clown
Are legend to our human childhood lent,

Has vanished. No directional intent
We find in Newton's world, and so may drown
When looking into what no more has meant
A certitude—the sky below the town?

I favor maps that put the southern pole
At top, that prompted one perhaps may be
To question our directionality.
But what will happen to our "upward" goal?

There's neither up nor down, and so the role
That heaven, hell will play might crazily
Careen and make you dizzy—- first with glee,
Then—hearken! For how hard the bell must toll

That has ungyroscoped the striving soul!
Within remained the unmapped balance: we,

A swaying center, find no "height" that He
Might live in. Grand, though, that expanding (w)hole!

Heav'n, earth, and hell—no more the simple three
Will spatial planning-kit provide, pardee.
Two zeroes we attach: infinity.

(64) The Square

Furnes

Capriciously by what-has-been outspread
Of rage and uproar; motley disarray
That went with the condemned on deathward way;
By stall and shack, the fairground-barker's cry,
And by the stately duke who's riding by,
The high-and-mighty Burgundy

(That background, all-embracingly):

The square will always ask you in, to see
How wide the distant windows are; and how
The entourage will, slow and calm, allow
Itself to be reshaped, made orderly

In space along a shop-lane. Gables rise
Of little homes that everything would view;
The tow'rs, made shy, to their own silence true,
Stand measureless behind in lonely wise.

(64) Reply

Within a centered town and one that winds
I've led my life. The latter I could tame
To something smaller that would feel the same
As that of childhood, closer, where one finds

Coherence (ev'n the shutting of the blinds
I had disliked, supposing it a shame
To separate oneself: let friends by name
Through windows greet me! Little things one
    minds ...).

I walk and cannot drive, and so the space
Around my home became a village-place.
The skies are cloudy theater. Each hill

And valley make me daily rise and fall.
Variety in little room is all.
The mind may world the air with windy will.

(65) Quai du Rosaire

Bruges

The lanes convey a quiet walk-along
(One thinks of people who, recovering,
Recalling, seek what once the view would bring);
Each lane that to the square will come, may long

Await another which, with single pace,
Will walk athwart an eve-clear water-place
Wherein the more surroundings milder grow
In-hanging worlds of mirroring will show
More real than upper things: the best, below.

This town, did it not vanish? Now you'll say
(According to a law we cannot know)
It wakes and is—in the transfigured—clear,
As if the life within were not so queer;
The gardens, plentiful, will ripen here;
Past quick-lit windows, right for small café,
'Tis dancing time in the estaminet.

Above, what stays?—the quiet, I divine,
Enjoying slowly, nothing to decry,
Grape after grape in mellow evening wine
Of glockenspiel that's hanging in the sky.

(65) Reply

The blending of the best in reverie
Is imaged in the underwater deep
That, outline smoothing, soothed me with a sleep
Unfallen into more than mirror-sea.

An emblem, this, of childhood memory.
What with my nature didn't well agree
I edited away: a cliff too steep
Would quickly to a soft declivity
Of lesser hindrance turn by dreamer-plea.

The peace of origin awoke in me:
The seaweed and the reeds; would Miriam weep
Supposing she was hoping that the neap
Tide would ensure the rise and fall would be
More equal now, and so would never sweep
The babe away when waves would upward creep?
Observe your vigil: long and tenderly.
The palace matron who would Moses keep
Was so enhanced by what had happened, she
Would to the true belief of Hebrews leap
And turn to heaven for eternity.

(66) Convent of Béguines

St. Elizabeth Convent, Bruges

I

There isn't anyone to guard the gate;
The bridge lends ready access, to and fro;
In olden elm-court all may safely wait
And feel no longer any need to go
Out of their houses, save on narrow way
To church, if they a better notion may
Attain of why their love was great and dear.

And there they kneel, with linen covered, pure,
And so alike one pattern would assure
The myriad vision that so deep and clear
As mirror served, where pillars order lend,
While voices ever higher will ascend
Along the path of song; so might they throw
A final word whenever notes won't go
Up to the angels. They return it not.

So those below are quiet in their thought
When rising, walking. And they silent reach,
While nodding to the glad receivers, each
With hallowed water that to heated brow
Will coolness (mouth remaining pale) allow.

They go, both hanging back and holding back,
Across that narrow little path again,

The tranquil young, the old that something lack—
One woman, old, delaying somehow then.
Their homes, when reached, they quickly silent
    make.
At times, through elms appearing, these will show
The purity of loneliness awake
That in a little pane of glass may glow.

II

But what is mirrored by the windowpanes
That, myriad, from the church on courtyard shine?
Gleam, countergleam, and quiet blend in state,
Perturb, grieve, drink, indeed exaggerate,
Fantastically age, like aged wine.

There lie, and there's no telling from what side,
Outer on inner, and eternity
On aye-surrender, wider over wide;
Unused and dark and blinding, leadenly.

There stays, amid the wavering décor
Of summer day, the gray old winter wore:
As if there stood with gentle, patient mind
An unconstrained and waiting He, behind,
And, weeping, an awaiting She, before.

(66) Reply

So Rilke, wise, will enter, readily,
The mind where Flemish nuns, awaiting, live:
Their world a pearl, because a purgative.
My poverty my pride—to this may we
Who follow Sufi wisdom tribute give.

The leather strip to the phylactery
Conjoined the Jew will 'round his finger thrice
Enwind, in token of the wedding he
Enjoys: the One will so the soul entice.

The trees will make me tall, the sky more tall
Than these; yet as a candle must I burn,
So have regard for those who would return
To that from whence arose their will to yearn.
Yet moments hold me, hold me most of all.

(67) The Mary Procession

Ghent

From every tower, rivers of it surge:
Upwelling metal, and so thickly massed—
As if the lanes below the bronze had cast
In dazzling day-mold of their shape to merge.

And on the edge, well-hammered, lofty, then
The walkers, motley-bound, come to the fore
Of graceful maidens and the new young men:
It pounded forceful waves and drove and bore,
Restrained but by the unpredictable
Weight of the banners, and a certain pull
Invisible as hand of God in air,

And suddenly, of kindred impulse full,
Stirred by the rise of censer upward, scared,
The flying seven that in peril fared
And at their chains of silver tore.

Surrounding ropes, the slope of urging crowd:
Awhile they halted, then they rushed and rolled:
Chryselephantine, see, it's coming near!
The canopy is raised and will appear
By balconies; asway, it's hung with gold.

They recognize, above the wide of white
Carried, and clad in Spanish garb, the best,
The olden statue with the small, hot, light

Face, and the child, by arm embraced, at rest.
They kneel more deeply when it comes to sight.
In glory crowned, unwittingly grown old,
It woodenly the blessing yet can hold:
That gesture grand will the brocade enfold.

But while it's passing by the ones who bow
(They're shyly looking upward from below),
An upward movement of each curving brow
The Virgin to her worshipers would show,
Determined, arrogant, and unrestrained:
They are amazed, consider while they stand,
Then hesitating leave. She has contained

Within herself the steps of all the stream
And goes, alone, on well-known ways at hand
Toward the bell-tow'r, the cathedral-gleam,
On hundred shoulders borne, hers to command.

(67) Reply: Serving the Virgin

Ovidian distichs

/xx /xx /xx /xx /xx /x
/xx /xx /   /xx /xx /

Framed by acacias and crazy-quilt house-walls thick-covered with creepers,
    Children on basketball courts, playing two separate games,

Barely outshout or out-sing (the Acropolis tow'ring above them)
    Birds on the branches, or loud pupils we hear from within.

Chanting the verses in unison, keeping identical cadence—
    Sounds that, we fancy, will rise up to the virginal fane.

Panathenaical pilgrims to chryselephantine Athena
    Offered the Lady their love, awe, apprehension, and hope

Twenty-five centuries past. And the Parthenon, built for the Lady,
    Shows to five waiters and two customers, mid-afternoon

Restaurant patrons, a view picture-windowed in full panorama.
    One has a cell-phone, valise, desktop computer, and pen.

He is conversing in querulous tones with a troublesome client,
    Helped by the helmeted war goddess of practical arts.

Now, though, we live in a time when the Lady herself needs defending.
    Even her lovers, alas!—kindly, but highly unwise—

Hoping to keep from collapse the poor Parthenon, added great iron
    Clamps but neglected to pour coatings of lead as the old

Builders of Hellas had done to bar rust (a molybdochoesis).
    Rust then expanded each clamp, splitting and shattering stone.

She who had beaten Poseidon in miracle working put up with
    One more calamity, *plus* cannonballs, gunpowder-fire,

Pious fanatic erasure of sculptural carving, Lord Elgin's
    Plundering, soot, acid rain. So is the Virgin ill-served.

(68) The Island

North Sea

I

The flood the road in shoals had wiped away,
And all appears alike on every side;
The little island, though, will always stay
Shut-eyed, for the confusing dikes abide

About the habitants, who in a sleep
Are born, that lets them switch their worlds around
In quiet, for they rarely make a sound,
Each sentence like an epitaph, to keep

For something that upswum and was unknown,
What unexplained arrived and would remain;
And so is all their gazes will maintain

From childhood on quite unapplied, upthrown,
Too big and inconsiderate, rough-grown:
It overtires their drive to stay alone.

II

As if it lay in circle-crater drowned
Upon a moon, each yard is dammed about;
Dressed all alike the gardens wait around
As orphans, hair smooth-combed. They're all worn
    out

Because the storm has folk so roughly raised:
Day after day the fear of death it brought.
They sit indoors and stare, and have appraised
What in the mirror slant on dresser thought

May bring of what is strange. A son will go
Before the door at evening, playing, slow,
Tones on harmonica that weep, belike—

A tune that he in distant harbor heard;
The shape arises of a sheep that stirred,
Big, threatening, upon the outer dike.

III

Near is the Inner, and all else is far—
This Inner pushing, urging, and each day
With overflow, there's more than it can say.
The island is a much too little star

That space had failed to note—disturbed, no word,
In its unwitting mode of being—fear—
So that it, underlit and overheard,
Alone

In order that this all an end might reach,
Darkly upon a self-invented way
Sought out, to go, not found within the play
Of planet, sun, or systems that we teach.

(68) Reply

I

"The Island" is an emblematic head
That holds no conversation with the dead.
How trapped one feels in a community
Of heavy bodies where no room can be.

In vain would we perpetuate what's vital
In midst of ailing organs in recital.
Not strange that I am driven to invent
A Colloquy with Singers Heaven-Sent.

In poems I converse with those I laud:
Mickiewicz, Rilke, Goethe, and with God.
A genius, I decide, is but a jinn

With fine essential flame awake within,
Not flooded out, by dike-walls quite confined.
And you can be one, too, if you've a mind.

II

The Heian kingdom of the Middle Age
Distinctive was for poet and for sage:
In daily lyrics did the Japanese
Nobility converse, and learn, and please.

So Wordsworth-Coleridge, and so Pound with Yeats
A friendship found that never age abates.
Thus Goethe, Schiller, felt in skies above
The lore of life: "no rescue but in love."

In Rilke, second strophe, we can hear
In broken-toned harmonica the clear
And urgent wail that summons from the deep,

A friend to waken from a numbing sleep.
A hundred verses' thunder let resound,
A thousand poems rouse the wind around!

III

The sudden puzzle-gap where phrasing failed
Portrays the writer in a crater jailed.
We need, at times, the quiet that we chose
When deafened by the sounding brass of prose.

The sandbank and the shallows reft of trees
Will make it hard for stirring breath of breeze
To bring the courage of the calling bird
Who means a mate should come if she has heard!

I have the only poet-heart I know
That must take part, if it would live and grow,
In colloquies where lyric-letters glow
Or else

(69) The Courtesans' Graves

They lie amid their lengthened hair,
Withdrawn into their brown and sunken faces.
The eyes, if closed or not, too filled with distance.
Mouth, skeleton, and flower. In the mouths
The teeth are smooth as might be travel-chessmen
Of ivory in rigid lines arranged.
And slender bones, and yellow pearls, and blossoms,
And hands; a tunic, faded garment woven
Above the heart that's fallen in. However,
Amid the rings and talismans well-shapen
Of stones the blue of eyes (a love-remembrance),
The quiet crypt remains of ancient ladies,
To vaulted roof piled high with petaled roses.
Again the yellow pearls, the loose, unfastened,
The terracotta vessels where the swell
With their own image was adorned, green potsherds
Of ointment vases, where the fragrance wafted,
And shapes of little deities: house altars,
Hetaera-heaven, with the gods delighted.
A sash undone, a flattened scarabaeus,
And little figures of a race of giants,
And lips that laugh, and dancing folk and runners,
And golden fibers, little bows well suited
For amulets of beast- and bird-pursuers;
Long pointed needles, dainty things domestic;
And one round fragment, background carmine-
    colored,
Displays no sable entryway inscription
But steed-legs of quadriga tense and tautened.

Again the blooms, the pearls unrolled for ages,
The brightened thighs enframing little lyre;
Between the veils like gentle cloudlets falling,
As if from shoe-cocoon they'd just departed,
The lightsome butterfly of tiny anklet.

And so they lie, with motley objects crammed,
Stones, costly things, and toys, and house
     equipment,
And shattered trifles (random things detaching),
And darken, as a river-bottom would.

They had been riverbeds,
Above which in the waves, the brief and rapid
(That sought their goal, to join the life hereafter),
The bodies of so many boys dashed falling,
And in the ones of men the streams rushed onward.
And sometimes broke the youths from out the
     mountains
Of childhood, and with timid fall went under,
And played with sundry things on river-bottom,
Till on their feelings would that fall lay hold:

And then they filled with shallow, clearer water
The breadth entire of all the way so widened,
And set up eddies in the deeper places;
As never hitherto, the shores they mirrored,
And far-off cries of birds, and meanwhile high
The starry nights, that nowhere will be closing,
In heaven grew, above that sweetest land.

(69) Reply

The test of lyric mastery, triumphant,
The poet passed: the hearer smiling-crying.
We might have thought the listing of the objects,
Of body-parts immixed with random fragments
Of female finery and house equipment
As *vanity of vanities* would function,
A portrait: skull with candle dripping slowly
While someone looking gloomy and reclusive
Would think of what might nevermore be mended
And try to find a comfort in the Bible.

But how transformed by Her, the ever living,
The boys and youths and men with river blended!
When Goethe sang the Journey of Muhammad,
He paralleled our Eden granted now.

(70) Orpheus. Eurydice. Hermes

'Twas rocky wonder-structure for the souls.
Like silent silver ore they wandered forth
As arteries through dark. Between the roots
The blood rushed up, to humans moving on,
And heavy, in the dark, as porphyry—
The only red.

And craggy rocks were there
And insubstantial woods. Void-vaulting bridges;
That gray and widening and blinded pond
That overhung its fundament afar
As rainy heaven over landscape hangs.
Between the meadows, gentle in forbearance,
Appeared the paling strip, the only pathway,
As one long pallid surfacing laid down.

Along that single pathway did they come.

The first, the slender man, blue-mantle-clad,
Who looked ahead in muteness though impatient.
His tread consumed the way unchewed in big
And hefty bites, the while his hands hung down,
Closed, heavily, from out the folds of clothing,
And knew no longer of the lightsome lyre
Which with the left hand intertwined had grown
As tendriled rose vine with a bough of olive.
His senses felt as if they had been split:
The gaze would, houndlike, run, anticipating,
Then turn around, come back, then further, farther,

Stay waiting at the bending of the road,—
His hearing, though, held back, like an aroma.
At times it seemed to him as if it reached
As far as where the other two were walking
Who had to follow this entire ascent.
Then it was echo, merely, of his treading
And wind that blew his cloak which were behind
        him.
He said, though, to himself: They're coming, still;
Out loud he said it, heard the echo dying.
They came indeed—just two they were,
Who went with fearful gentleness. And might he
But turn around (if looking back were not
The undermining of the whole endeavor
That sought accomplishment), he would behold
The two so gentle, following him, silent:

The god of going, he the message-herald,
The travel-hood above the shining eyes,
Thin staff before the body stretching outward,
And beating pinions at the ankle-joints;
And to the hand, the left, surrendered: *she.*

The so much loved, for whom more dole resounded
From lyre than heard from any wailing woman.
It was a world of dirge created where
Was all retained: the forest and the vale,
And path and village, river, mead, and beast;
So that around this mourning-world as 'round
The other earth, a sun was circulating;
A constellated heaven, quiet, went,

A mourning-heaven, every star displaced—:
She, so much loved.

She walked on, guided by a godly hand,
Her gait held in by ceremental ribbons,
Unsure, a gentle tread, without impatience;
Within herself, as one with hope of higher,
Who thought not of the man who strode before her.
She, self-contained. Because her having-died
Had filled her as with fullness.
Like to a fruit, with sweetness, dark, replete,
So was she full with greatness of her death,
That was so new that she could nothing grasp.

For she was in a new virginity,
Not touchable, her maidenhead enclosed
As of a youthful blossom toward the evening,
Her hands to marriage dishabituated
So that the guiding touch, unending-tender,
Even of him, the gentlest god, the herald,
Made her feel ill—too intimate, too near.

No longer could she be that lady blond
Who echoed in the poets' song at times,
No more the air and isle of ample bed,
And the possession of her man no more.

She had been loosened as the lengthened hair,
Surrendered as the lightly falling rain,
Divided as a hundredfold supply.

She now was root.

And so, when suddenly
The god restrained her and with painful outcry
Pronounced the words: Look, he has turned
    around—,
She grasped it not and, quietly, said *Who?*

Afar, and dark before the brightened exit
A certain someone stood: the countenance
One could not recognize. He stood and saw
How on the little strip of meadow path,
The eyes with mourning filled, the god, the herald,
Turned silent 'round, her form to follow after,
Who had returned the selfsame way she came,
Her gait hemmed in by ceremental ribbons,
Unsure, a gentle tread, without impatience.

(70) Reply: Anna Akhmatova's "Lot's Wife"

with **Comment**

Lot's Wife

*But Lot's wife looked behind her and became
a pillar of salt.*
—Book of Genesis

He followed God's envoy. Big, mighty, and shining,
The righteous man led her along the black hill.
His anguish was heard in loud words unrepining:
It isn't too late! Take another look still:

Behold the red towers of Sodom, your city,
The square and the court where you chanted and
    spun,
The windows, how empty; the house, tall and pretty,
Where children you bore, for a much-loving one.

She gazed and, enfettered with hurt that would kill
    her,
The pain-wasted eyes could no more gaze around.
Her body, now salt, was transparent, a pillar,
The quick-moving feet rooted fast to the ground.

And who will bemoan her, and who will regret her
Great loss with the vanishing glance that she took?
I know that my heart cannot ever forget her
Surrendering life to a lingering look.

Comment

It may at first appear the husband was
A murderer for cruel words that told
His wife, "Look back!" What if they'd "left her cold"?
At first they didn't, then they did, because

She died of having lived. We all enjoy
The minute—we would save it—and we can't.
Our lives are saline, fatal: Hamlet's rant,
Lear's, or a newborn's, prove me Chronos' toy.

Salt is our obelisk, dried ocean-tears.
We're water: molten Moment flows away.
"Love it," urged Heraclitus, but they say
A weeper, too, was he … Forgoing fears,

The wife: beholder-poet-heroine:
She liked, she looked. She thanked—she drank it in.

(71) Alcestis

There was the herald suddenly among them,
Tossed in, new contribution to the stew,
The wedding dinner, that was boiling over.
The drinkers didn't realize the entry
Of deity was hid, who held his nature
Supernal close to him, as mantle moistened,
And seemed as one of them, no matter which,
Just passing through. But suddenly a guest
Amid a conversation caught a glimpse:
The youthful master, up above, at table,
No more reclining, to a height was seized—
Now everywhere, and with the fullest essence,
Of alien strength a mirror—fearful claim!
Immediately—a clearing of the mixture—
Came quiet, only from below a jumping
Of muddled noise, and suddenly a downswing
Of patter falling, redolent in ruin
Of muffled or of unacknowledged laughter.
And then they recognized the slender god
And how he stood there, filled with inner mission
And unappeasable—they almost knew it.
And yet, when it was said, it more appeared than
Was knowable, beyond all understanding.
Admetus—he will die. When? At this hour.

But, shattering the shell of all his terror,
Admetus, hands in brave entreaty lifted,
Beyond enclosure, strove with god to bargain:
"Just for some years, a single year still youthful,

For months, for weeks, for only days, a few—
Ah! not for days, for nights—for merely one, then,
For just one night, for *this* one, just the one!"
The god denied him, and he cried aloud
And louder cried, could not hold back, and cried
As in her labor had his mother shouted.

And one approached him then, a woman, old,
The father, too, came near, the aged father;
And there they stood, the ancient, faded, baffled.
He, crying, as if nearer now than ever,
Observed them, then broke off, and sobbing said:
"Father,
Can what remains attach you vainly yet
To those old dregs that barely can be swallowed?
Go, pour them out! And you, you woman old,
Matron,
What have you still to do? You've given birth."
He held them both like sacrificial victims
In single grasp. At once, he let them go,
Dismissing them, with sudden insight, shining
And breathing deeply, calling: Creon! Creon!
And naught but this; and nothing but this name.
Yet in his countenance was something other—
A thing unmentioned, nameless, but awaited,
As he the youthful comrade, much belovéd,
Exhorted heatedly across the table:
"The old ones standing, look, they'll be no ransom;
They're quite used up, no good, and nearly worthless!
But you, at least, you, here, in all your beauty—"

But now he could no longer see his friend.
He stayed unmoving; one came near; 'twas *she*,
A little smaller than when last he'd seen her,
And slight, and sad, in pallid bridal garment.
The others are no more than lane or pathway:
By that, she's coming, coming—soon embraced in
His arms, that open painfully to clasp her.

He's waiting, and she speaks, but not to him.
She talks to God alone, and God— he listens,
They all, as if in God, intently hearing:

"None can be substitute for him. I'm *it*.
I'm substitute. For no one, at the end,
Is what I am. What's here for me of all
That I was, here? And that is why I'm dying.
Did she who set your mission never tell you
That every situation that is waiting
To Underworld belongs? I made my parting.
Parting after parting.
No mortal parted more. And so I left,
That all which under him is dead and buried
Who's now my spouse may scattered be and vanish.
Lead me away now. I will die for him."

As on high sea upleaps the wind surrounding,
So came the god as if to one who'd perished
And suddenly was distant from her husband,
To whom God, in a little hidden signal,
The hundred lives of this our earth was granting.
Admetus plunged in tumult toward them both

And groped as in a dream. They'd moved away
Already to the entrance, where the women
In tears were thronging. He a moment looked
Up at the maiden's face, and viewed it turning,
Lit with a smile, and bright as hope, that nearly
A promise meant: ascending from the deep of
Death to return to him, the living—

Quickly
His face he covered with his hands, and knelt,
That he no more might see, beyond that smiling.

(71) Reply

Methought I saw my late espoknséd saint
Brought to me like Alcestis from the grave,
Whom Jove's great Son to her glad Husband gave,
Rescued from death by force though pale and
*   faint.*
. . . . .
Love, sweetness, goodness, in her person shin'd
So close, as in no face with more delight. . . .
                    —John Milton, "Methought I Saw. . ."

St. Anne had smiled so, Bacchus, John the Baptist,
And she that pilgrims 'round the world would travel
To view: the Leonardo-felt enigma.

The painter's mother, taken from him early,
Is matron of his heart, in whom the Father
Will speak, recalling god-light in her smiling.

Alcestis, faithful wife, remains a maiden,
The one who beckons, from the night to greet him,
As *Ave maris stella!* prayed the sailor.

His wife, long-mourned, did Milton see while
    dreaming.
She vanished when he wakened, and his blindness,
Her face now gone, made living doubly darker.

(72) Birth of Venus

This morning after—frightful! what a night
That came and passed—with shouting, trouble,
     uproar!—
The sea entire broke open with a cry.
And as the cry closed in upon itself
From paling day, the heavens' open-moment,
Downfalling in the muted fish-abyss—
The sea gave birth.

From early sun forth shimmering, the hair-foam
Of wider shame of waves, and on the shore
The maiden, white, stood up, bewildered, wet.
As youthful, green, a leaf will touch itself
And, stretching, open out what was rolled up,
The body in the cool was slow-unfolded
Both inwardly and toward the untouched dawnwind.

Like moons in clarity the knees uprising
Sank back in cloudy borders of the thighs.
The narrow shadow of the calves withdrew,
The feet were lighter when they slightly tensed,
The joints lived even as the eager throats
Of drinkers.

In harbor-hollow chalice lay the body
As new-found fruit enclasped in childish hand.
Within the narrow goblet of the navel
Was all the darkness of that gleaming life.
Above would hover, light, the little wavelets

And, steady, overflow it toward the loins
Where now and then a quiet streaming was.
Light-pierced, however, still without a shadow,
Mindful of birchen grove in early April,
Warm, empty, and unhidden, the pudenda.

Now stood the lively balance of the shoulders
In equilibrium on upright body
That from the water like a springtime fountain
Rose, wavered, falling then on slender arms,
More speedy yet the rushing fall of hair.

Next, very slowly passing by, the face:
From interrupted darkness of her bending
Into a clear, symmetric, lifted being.
Below, held somewhat back, the upright chin.

Now, with the neck extended as a ray
And as a flower stem with sap arising,
The arms would also be in pleasure spread
Like swans when they are looking for the shoreline.

Then came into this body's darkened dawntime
What seemed the breathing, first, of morning wind.
In tender networks of arterial branches
A whispering occurred; the blood began
To rush across the depth of newer places.
And now it grew, this wind: it threw itself
With fullest breath into the new-grown breasts
And filled them, and impelled itself in them,
So that like sails, which were with distance filled,
They urged the lightsome maiden to the strand.

Thus land she reached, the goddess.

And behind her,
Who now across the shoreline, young, was running,
To the unfolding noon were opened up
The flow'rs and grasses, warm, bewildered,
As if they'd been embraced. She went, she ran.

At noon, however, in the heaviest hour,
Climbed up sea again on high and threw
A dolphin on the place where she had been:
Dead, red, and open.

(72) Reply

hendecasyllabics

/ x / xx / x / x / x

Sun-god oracle? Here behold your Dolphin.
First, a crew to the holy place conducting
Where they priestly would be, Apollo's honor,
All at once he was altered! In amazement,
Sailors followed; the Dolphin wisely guided:

Picked a nebulous rift, where later sybil
(Pythia—in the older time her title)
Vapors breathing, would emanate in lessons
Veiled-revealing, enigmas to unriddle.
Mist-delphinian: oracle at Delphi.

(1)

Dead and bloody, the *delphos* thrown by ocean.
Let's recall that Ourános, god of heaven,
Was deprived by his son of privy member—
Knife-revenge by the wrathful rebel Kronos!
Fell the genital, fertilized the water.

Then arose Aphrodite (Roman Venus):
Progeny of a passion truly brutal—
Loose and dallying, she, in later mythos.
Love and *bloody*—entwined from wild beginnings
(Theme we needn't develop any further).

(2)

Next we turn to the sad prophetic apple
On the surface of which was "Beauty" written.
Eris (Discord) had thrown the fruit in anger
When she wasn't invited to the wedding
Thetis, Peleus held (Achilles' parents).

Who, most beautiful, will deserve the fruit-prize:
Aphrodite, Athena, maybe Hera?
Paris, prudent, was told to judge the contest:
Hera offered the kingship of the world-realm;
Wise Athena, her prudent skill in battle.

Last, the love of the lady all considered
First in beauty among existing women
Aphrodite would offer Paris. Tempted,
Her he chose, and he won the Trojan Helen:
Blood and burning would end our second legend.

(3)

Venus (change to the later Latin naming)
Was the mother of pious, grave Aeneas.
Him had Jupiter chosen as the founder,
After years, of the warlike Roman nation.
Venus, though, of the love motif was mindful.

She would guide the reluctant boat to Carthage,
Where Queen Dido, enamored of Aeneas,
Rescued him from a storm the foam-born started.

Dido rescued the nearly shipwrecked sailor,
Took him then to a cave for evening banquet.

Angry Jupiter couldn't grant approval:
What a frivolous, trivial intermission!
Scolding, lashing the man to pious duty,
He commanded: Depart, and leave the lady!
So he did. On her flaming pyre she perished.

Thus we've ended our three delphinian lessons.
Roma—nothing but Ámor written backward.
Mars our Venus would lead away from Vulcan.
So the fatal is lover of the fertile.
They're entwined, though we mainly fail to see it.

(73) The Vase of Roses

You saw them, angry, flare; two youths you saw,
Tight-clasped into a ball, and who knows why.
It was but hate, and rolled about the ground,
One animal, new-felled by stinging bees;
Mere actors, strutting-high exaggerators,
Like steeds enraged, collapsing, breaking down,
With rolling eyes, and baring of the teeth
As if the skull were splitting from the lips.

But now you know how this forgot itself:
Before you stands the vase with roses filled
Made unforgettable because replete
With uttermost of being and inclining,
Restraint, surrender-never, standing-fast,
That would be ours: an uttermost for us.

A soundless life, a going-up unending,
Room-needing, yet not taking room from that
Room which diminishes the things around,
Almost not-outlined, something set apart
And purely inner, strange in tenderness,
Exhaling radiance—to the very edge.
Do we know anything resembling this?

And then like this: that feeling should arise
When flower petals flower petals touch?
And this: that one will open like a lid
And underneath lie other eyelids waiting
And closed, as if they, in a tenfold sleep,

Had needed to tamp down the pow'r of vision.
And then, this most of all: that through these petals
The light must penetrate. From myriad heavens
They're slowly filtering that drop of darkness
In whose gleamed fire the yet bewildered bundle
Of pollen vessels, agitated, towers.

As for the movement in the roses, look:
Gestures from such a little nook unfolding
They'd be invisible, did not their rays
Not run all helter-skelter into world-all.

Look at the white one that has, happy, blossomed
And stands there in the large and open leaves
Recalling Venus upright on the seashell;
And this one, reddening as if confused,
That tries to bend across to one who's cooler;
The cooler one unfeelingly withdraws
And, like the cold one, stands, in self enwrapt,
Among the open ones that all are shedding;
And *what* they shed, a light and heavy thing,
As if it mantle, burden, wing, and mask
Might be, that vary as the flow'rs themselves,
And *how* they shed, as if before a loved one.

There's naught they cannot be: this yellow one
That open, hollow lies—was it not skin
Of fallen fruit, the yellow hue the same,
And, too, the gathered juice of orange-red?
And was the rising just too much for this one
Since in the air the pink without a name

Took on the bitter aftertaste of lilac?
Could this one of batiste portray a dress
In which yet tender, breath-warm, hides the blouse,
The both of them together thrown aside
In morning shadow of old woodland bath?
And this one here, the opal porcelain,
As fragile as a shallow china cup
And filled with tiny, brightly-colored moths—
And that one, nothing holding but itself.

Aren't they all themselves alone containing,
If self-containment means: the world without,
The wind and rain and patience of the spring
And guilt and trouble and enfolded fate
And darkness of the evening on the earth
Up to the wander-clouds, their going, coming,
To the vague distant influence of stars,
To change into a hand with in-ness filled.

Now lies it carefree in the open roses.

(73) Reply

Who'll change the fire to rose and tree
Can charm the world from harm to free
The soul, than cypress deeper green,
By fragrance rendered melody.

The petals bold, supremely seen,
Are both the castle and the queen
And testify as well to all
That centuries of tending mean.

The nightingale aroma call
Will bid approach the palace hall
That he a love may wild outpour
Distilled in tones that mildly fall.

The secret in her breathing more
Will rouse in fountaining to soar
The sound of sufi bird of eld
Than ever told the olden lore.

From love undampened, never quelled,
The depth of aural breath can meld
With Rhoda's own auroral scent
As gold and gem the craftsmen weld.

The álif in creation meant
That heaven strength would not relent
In artery and heart of fire
Where blood of willing welling went.

Euglena and amoeba higher
Would climb in towering desire
Till Sheba and her Nightingale
In Eden bower might respire.

If thorn be warden, winter pale
Affray awhile in icy mail,
The cypress needn't sigh, for we
Shall feel the May that cannot fail.

NEW POEMS II,
TRANSLATED WITH
VERSE REPLIES

(74) Archaic Torso of Apollo

We had not known of that unheard of head
Where apples of the eyes had ripened, though
His torso's candelabra-like—white glow;
The gaze, half turned away, inhibited,

Yet steady gleams. Not otherwise the bend
Of breast could blinding dazzle, or the loins
In softly turning form a smile that joins
Them to the center that could life expend.

The stone would else be over-short, design
Distorted under shoulders' bright incline,
And glimmer not as fur on beast of prey:

Nor forth could breathe, a burst of stellar ray
From borders all. That widened gaze no strife
Allows evading. You must change your life.

(74) Reply

The noble, simple, quiet grandeur found
When Winckelmann a statue would observe
Depended on perception of the curve
Recalling swelling seas no man would sound.

That roundness had a sweet maternal ease
Where bounty of the ocean would abound;
The bodies molten seemed: each contour wound
In smoothened surging, soothing urgencies.

See, here, the gleam and dazzle and the star,
The candelabrum and the glimmering?
The water-mother turned to fiery king.

The statue and the god have been remanned.
We hear the silent strike of a command:
Arise, and be as the eternal are.

(75) Cretan Artemis

Wind of headlands, foothills: wasn't her
Forehead like an object swathed in light?
Smooth opposing light-beast wind astir,
Did you form her, garment bright

Shaping for the breasts, the unaware,
Like a changeable presentiment?
Meanwhile she, with wise, all-knowing air,
Girded for the distant, coolness lent,

Stormed with hordes of nymphs, near each a hound,
Testing out the bows they'd firmly bound,
Straps high-fastened, tight of girth,

Sometimes from their settlements afar
Summoned, wrathful, where the perils are,
By the cries attending birth.

(75) Reply: Artemis and Apollo

alcaic

The isle of Delos rose at a god-command,
A palm-tree planted deep in her sacred lake,
      In order that the holy mother
      Leto could lean on the trunk while birthing

Apollo, Artemis, the lacustrine twins.
The goddess-child came first. With a kindly hand
      She helped assure her blue-eyed, blond-haired
      Brother's delivery'd be less painful.

The island-theme was purification. Here
You'd neither be allowed to be born nor die.
      But chapel, temple, fane abundant—
      Isis, Apollo, and Dionysus—

Were multitude. The Artemis altar's might
Did not diminish that of the phalloi bold
      Atop their poles, the long-neck'd rooster,
      Maenad, Silenus, the nymphs, and Hermes

That filled the Dionysian shrine. When Greeks
Envisioned, with Egyptians, a blended god,
      The new Sarápis had resplendent
      Powers of Hapi and dark-bright Wésir.

In later centuries, when the Grecian boats
Approached, the grieving breezes appeared to cry:
      "The gods, the gods are gone forever!"—
      Sinking the heart and the hope of sailors.

(76) Leda

When he was entered by the god in need,
The latter nearly feared to find him fair;
He let himself, bewildered, vanish there.
But soon betrayal bore him into deed

Before the feeling of untested-yet
Being he grasped. The open maiden, drawn,
Had recognized the one who came in swan,
Had guessed the single thing he meant to get

From her, bewildered in opposing and
Unable to protect it. Down came he
And pressed his neck past ever weaker hand

And that which was within set, flowing, free.
Then first he felt glad feathers fledged and soon
Became true swan, he knew, within her womb.

(76) Reply

Already was the god new-born before
The one he entered ever children bore.
The mysteries of love and woman gave
What would redeem, and lift beyond, and save.

How fall'n, how changed became the swan in Yeats,
Who, power-crazed, no cruelty abates;
We rather are directed to apprise
The victim, dropped, as having seen the skies.

Return to Rilke, should you wish to be
Recomforted with kinder deity:
His power will he milden when the hour
Will make god wiser in the maiden-bow'r.

So poets' different ways of reading myth
Will show us clearly what we're dealing with.

(77) Dolphins

Actual beings, who their like divine
Lent the wherewithal to dwell and grow,
Felt by many a relation-sign
Friends in loosened realms where god would go
Streaming and with dripping tritons climb:
For the animal had shown, in time,
More than muted, muffled, dull-as-mud
Fishes, kindred blood to human blood,
And to distant humans had inclined.

Group, where each above the other leapt
Gaily came, as feeling-currents gleam:
Warm, devoted, fond, their order kept
Form that might a journey-wreath beseem;
Lightly linked about the curving bay
As a border, vase enrounding, may,
Carefree, blest, and safely they would play;
Upright, frenzied, leaping, widely ranging,
Diving motion with the wave exchanging,
Which would bear the trireme-craft away.

And the sailor took the new-acquired
Friend within his danger-life alone,
For the friend designed (the much desired)
Gratefully a world, and then would own
That the friend loved garden, god, and tone;
Year-scheme quiet, deep, and star-inspired.

(77) Reply: Alexander Pushkin's "Arion" with Comment

Arion

Within that craft, the crew we were:
While some the sail would gladly trim
The others with an easy vim
Deep plunged the mighty oar. No stir:
The helmsman shrewdly moved the wheel,
The heavy bark in silence led,
And I, with hopeful, carefree head,
Sang to the mariners. We'd feel
A sudden whirlwind up ahead!
The helmsman and the crew were lost:
I, bard of mystery, sing on,
By storm upon the shoreline tossed
To chant my former hymns on high:
The sodden robe on rock I dry
Below the light, before it's gone.

Comment

I'll tell you more: while on the boat,
Each Orphean and warning note
I chanted to the one I love
By wiser guidance from above
The dolphins charmed, who circled 'round
And whirled about the artful sound.
The largest me to seaside bore
Where longing-warmth might song restore:
In glory to the great "I am,"

I chanted then the dithyramb.
When pirate Dionysus lashed
To oaken mast, he unabashed
The pole made sprout: behold! with vines
The god the livened tree entwines.
The sailors leap: they're dolphins now
And proudly crowd around the prow.

(78) The Isle of Sirens

When to those who were his welcome guests,
Late, when they'd inquire, at end of day,
Of his journeyings, and peril-tests,
He'd report, he never knew that they

Found it fearful and with sudden word
Turned away, that they as well as he
In the quiet blueness of the sea
Would behold the golding isles unstirred,

Which, when gazed on, what a danger made,
Now surrounding!—perils heralded
Not in raging, where they'd once been laid:
Silent over sailors they will spread,

Men who know that in that golden scene
On an isle one heard a singing sound—
On the rudder one at times might lean,
Girded round

By the silence that the mile-lengths wide
Holds entire, and into ears unmanned
Breathes, as if the quiet's other side
Were the singing no one can withstand.

(78) Reply

Had we vision keen and feeling of
All that ordinary lives outpour
We the growing grass would hear in love
And the squirrel's heartbeat know, adore:

Then, however, we should also die,
Die upon our hearing what a roar
Will on farther side of silence lie.
So George Eliot has told, and more.

When in *Middlemarch* I read her word,
Sudden shock I felt of seeming fright:
Loved I not the silence that I heard
Every night?

Then I realized what pow'rs defend
Human frailty from the quiet foe.
Gentle stream-rush in the ear, a friend
Half-unheard must forth, abiding, go.

So the body guards the mind she aids
And, as well, the other way around;
Soothing music from awareness fades
Of the blood-engendered friendly sound.

(79) Lament for Antinoüs

None of you here could preserve the Bithynian boy
(Holding back *some*how the wave, that the victim
    might live).
True, I had spoiled him. Indeed it was this, silly joy,
That would but heaviness lend, and bewilderment
    give.

Who really knows how to *love*? There is no one can
    do it:
Trouble unending I've made, fatal damage have done.
Now he is one of the gods of the Nile, and I rue it;
Knowing not which, I can't think of approaching that
    one.

Mad ones, you tossed him up high, all the way to the
    stars;
Did you intend I should ask where the vanished
    might dwell?
Best call him simply a dead man: he'd like it quite
    well:
No more events of the kind that humanity mars.

(79) Reply

Antinoüs to early death would go
In River Nile when he untimely fell
Or possibly was murdered by a foe,
Or killed himself, as fertile-flooding spell.

The Emperor was overcome with woe
For his beloved, and a rage would swell
The breast, and lines with lyric tears would flow.
Though Egypt-style religion suited well

The deifying of the beauteous youth;
The king could barely view it as the truth.
He blamed himself, as if a baleful spell
He'd cast, to lonely life replying NO.

(80) The Death of the Beloved

Of death he knew what everybody knows:
It takes you to the place where no one cries.
His darling dies? Not torn away she goes,
No, gently loosened from the realm of eyes

And gliding over to the shades unknown,
And as he feels that those on high have now
Accustomed to her maid-smile moonlight grown,
And to her mode of being bow,

He seems so well acquainted with the dead
As if to every one of them he were
Related (let the people talk!) through her.

(Forget the people!) Lands were, in his head,
Well named: the well-laid-out, the ever-sweet.
He tested them: how would they suit her feet?

(80) Reply

He'd feel quite pleased with dramas of Japan
Where in a home the souls will come and go,
Accompanying bodied people so
As enemies might do, and comrades can.

In medieval Russian legends, too,
Worlds intermingle most agreeably:
In rural field a farmer you may see
Upon a devil's back. The georgic view

A moral holds: a demon has to work
And do his duty, hold your goal in view;
So harness the accosting fiend—and plow.

He'd best get sober, wipe away the smirk:
He'll thank you for the task he has to do
And be a steady steed, whom rule may cow.

(81) Lament for Jonathan

Ev'n kings no actuality command:
They vanish as an evanescent thing,
Although their impress, as on royal ring,
Is reproduced about the tender land.

But how indeed could *you*, that so began
With the initial of your heart,
So quickly cease? Warmth of my cheeks!—a man
That I could wish might through begetter's art
Arise to life, seed shine in him and sing.

Only a foreigner you had to fear,
While me, who lived within you, naught avails,
Who must restrain himself and tiding hear;
As wounded creatures to their lairs draw near,
I'd lay me down, with cries and wails:

For here and there, in my most hidden places
You seem resembling hair that's ripped away;
It grew in armpits and, for ladies' play,
In other secret spaces.

Before you, tangled senses everywhere
In me unraveled as a skein unwound:
I, looking up at you, became aware.
I now see nothing, vanished face, unfound.

(81) Reply

My body and my friend capacity
Contain which is one morning torn away.
The eyes that in the mirror nothing see
But waning of my spirit-being say
By shadow I'm replaced in empty day.

The strength I had is far, lethargic. Will
Must come to be by what it came to do.
And this I cannot feel, apart from you:
No motion, comrade vanished. Still.

We cannot live in silence. Quiet tone
A kindly nature placed in waiting ear;
'Tis company. But oh! my final fear—
It is to be a silent soul, alone.

(82) Consolation of Elijah

He had been doing this and that, the bond
And the neglected altar to rebuild;
The faith once flung away, on him unstilled
Came back and fell, and flaming, from beyond.
And more than hundreds then he'd wanted killed,
Mouths fouled with name of Baal, of evil fond,
Unhalted slaughter that gray evening still

Which with the stream, gray-rained, one ash-hue
        spanned.
The queen's own herald, though, arriving now,
Such workday, threatening, no more'd allow.
Then ran he like a madman through the land

Till underneath a broom-bush, wild to view,
As from an outcast burst, a cry outpoured
That in the waste land roared: Use me, O Lord,
No more: I'm split in two!

Then came an angel, who would cauterize
The ache with food that he would glad accept,
And long through waters, willow groves, he kept
Proceeding till the headlands would arise,

To whom the Lord descended, for his sake:
And not in storm, and not in riving split
Of earth, with heavy folds in fury lit
By empty fire, but—though 'twould shamefaced
        make

The deity above the settled flood
Outbroken—to the agéd one 'twas fit
To feel in soft uprushing of his blood
The message he, afraid and hid, would take.

(82) Reply

More apt our Quiet Wisdom tips
May give than brash apocalypse.
Crash-"rapture" they will rashly seek
Who are in definitions weak.
"Rapacity"—same Latin root—
But etymology is moot
For those who think a "raptor" fit
To turn away from "rapier" wit.

Do they who at some 'savior' gaped
Know "rapio" relates to "raped"?
A world in chaos-flame who'd end
That was to the Creation friend?

Loud violence we put aside
Who in Elias' calm abide.
Avow: it awes the inner ear
When guidance quietly is clear.

For joyful tidings, tranquil voice
Would be the vehicle of choice
The words he heard—as light!—to say:
Anoint Elisha. Now. Today.

The words declaring "Light let be"
Are wise: we hear them silently.
It had required no louder tone
To shout, for only God alone

Might hear, no other being made
As yet, who might for light have prayed.
Sun came to sate the waiting mind
That contemplated unconfined.

(83) Saul among the Prophets

Does the king regret debased desire?
No, a lofty look appeared in him
When his stalwart lad with psalming lyre
He had planned on tearing limb from limb.

Only when the Spirit on such ways
Him had overcome, asunder rent,
He within had felt no blessing rays,
And his blood in deepened darkness went
Superstitiously to Judgment Days.

When his mouth now rightly prophesied,
It was so the fugitive might hide.
Second vision, this, of prophet-eye:
Earlier, the king could prophesy,

Childlike, as if every artery
Issued sweet in lips of bronzen art:
All walked straight; the straightest one was he;
All had cried; his cry was from the heart.

Now he was no more than simple heap,
Burdens piled and dignities forsaken;
Mouth that no essential truth might keep,
Eave-trough whence the waters would be taken,
Borne away, ere he'd awaken.

(83) Reply

"Saul is among the prophets." If we read
These words proverbial, the fateful day
Of Samuel's anointing him we'll heed
And grateful in our mental world replay
Commemoratively the lyric lay.

That God anointed him confirmed would be,
Claimed Samuel, when Saul would later see
A group of prophets from a high place come
Who'd play upon the timbrel, flute, and drum.

He waited briefly, glimpsed them speedily:
A heart alive, that earlier was mute,
Replied with cries to timbrel, drum, and flute.
They had averred: a holy king was he.

One later day he viewed the group, but when
He called them, they withdrew: their halidom
He joyful joined with timbrel, flute, and drum.
That man was made the happiest of men!

In soul we find that Saul, by lyric borne
As wild-ox heightened with an upraised horn,
Could as none other value David's lyre.
Sad, when the once divine, then darkened fire
Had spirit disaligned from son-ray torn.

(84) Samuel's Appearance before Saul

The Endor woman shouted out, "I see—"
"See whom?" The king had seized her by the arm.
But what the staring one described would he
Behold before she'd end, and to his harm:

The one whose voice he'd taken in before.
"Why bother me? I want to sleep some more.
Would you, because the heavens laid a curse
Upon you, and the Lord is mute and gone,
Desire that I, by words, your fate reverse?
And should I count my teeth for you? They're all
I have ..." He vanished. And the woman cried;
Her face of woe she laid her hands upon,
As if indeed she'd seen him. "You will fall—"

And Saul, who in the time he fate defied,
Had towered over troops, a banner high,
Fell down. Ev'n to lament he could not try,
Defeat was not to be denied.

But she, who'd struck him down against her will,
Hoped he'd collect himself and just forget;
And when she heard that he a fast had set,
Went out and slaughtered food and baked her fill

And brought the meal to him, that he might eat;
He sat like one who has too much forgot:
All things, from start to finish—all unthought.
And like a youth he ate his evening treat.

(84) Reply

What you from me receive you see in dream.
As interlocutor and medium
My Endor I've unlocked, and they who come
Will wraithlike radiate beseeming gleam.

They speak your fate, embodying your will
And fear. A man an epic war must be.
A self-appointed sovran each, they still,
When wanting you to conquer or to flee,
May shift their shape and, wily, meld and merge,
Confounding deviltry and demiurge.
For wish and fear, alike in mirror-tricks,
Take on disguises that they try to fix
And roles that they with difficulty fill.

Deceit far less you find on Endor-night.
And why? Unloosed, the horses of the deep
Race upward, higher than our daytime sight,
And newly fortified by reason-sleep.

The sun is black that warms the under-realm,
The view that 'truth is light and clarity'
Belied. The bright-eyed pilot at the helm
Of mind? A proud, a drowsy one is he.

You call on Samuel? He'll nothing know
That he has not already said and you
Would like him to deny. The nightmare's true,
For so the quiet in your soul may show.

(85) The Prophet

Made by giant countenances wide,
Bright with shining fire, come from the course
Of a judgment (he not nullified)
Are the eyes that gazing yet abide
Under thickest brows. And now, inside,
Words are readying again with force,

Words not his (for what would be his own?
And, to spare the hearer, what a waste!)—
Others, hard: steel piece, or block of stone,
He would smelt—volcano, flaming-faced—

So's to throw them then, with ire that frowned
Down as he would utter curse on curse!
While his forehead, as of humble hound,
Sought to bear what would be worse

Till by God removed from there, assuaged:
He, He is the one they all would find
Should they keep those warning hands in mind
That will show Him as He is: enraged.

(85) Reply

Mirrored is the maker in the made.
Read the statement any way you will:
Sympathetic wit is here displayed,
Part-parodic, too, and unafraid,
Alternate responses to be weighed
Offering, delighted mind to fill.

Wrath, which eats a person up inside,
One more readily may tolerate
When in Father's higher eye espied;
Sanctified—that load, the over-great.

God feels better, and the Prophet, too,
Once from burden of the fire set free.
That is *one* emancipation true
To the Abrahamic writings three.

Sadly, all the thunder-stones downthrown
Stun the blamer, even as the blamed.
Till the mercy-doctrine can be shown
Heart-divinity is harmed—and shamed.

(86) Jeremiah

Tender was I then as early wheat ...
You, though, Who are one that frenzy breathes,
Charmed my heart, restrained, with alien heat.
Hear: it with a fire-of-lion seethes.

Bold the mouth You would for me presume
When I'd barely grown to be a youth:
It was but a wound—now bleeds, in truth,
Hapless year on hapless year in gloom.

Daily novel tones from me would sound
That, Insatiable, You would invent.
None could smite my lips to bite the ground.
None but You might silence-pow'r have sent.

When we have dispersed, perturbed, displaced,
And have lastly lost and gone astray,
Entering the peril of the heart,
Then, among the ruin-heap defaced,
I'll re-hear my voice that final day,
Which was but a howling from the start.

(86) Reply: Leçon de ténèbres

Lamentatio Jeremiae: Quo-
modo sedet sola civitas
Plena populo? The moral this
For a people causing awful woe
When it wronged itself, their bitter loss
Who the lesson of the Lord dismiss.

Hand of clay that's cleaving to the dust
Braver may become when once it must:
Fury is inhabiting the skies
Warning life-inhibitors unwise.

Humans who with steam will heat the seas
Hourly so pollute the ocean breeze:
Consequent tornado and typhoon
Veil the breaking day and rive the moon.

Time to write a jeremiad: I
See the threaded letters in the sky.
Life, behold, and death—a choice for you:
Tophet-smoke, or green and gold and blue.

(87) A Sibyl

Years ago they used to call her old.
Yet she stayed, and walked, and never faltered.
Same, the street she came along. They altered
Measure, and her age they reckoned, bold,

By the centuries, as of a wood.
At the same old spot she daily stood,
Black as citadel that's high and stout:
Hollow, as if ravaged and burnt out,

Unaware of words that yet abounded
Tumbling out despite the will they spurned;
She was flown-about, by these surrounded,
While the others homeward had returned,
Now behind their iris darkly sitting,
Finished for the evening, as was fitting.

(87) Reply

Who's dark behind the iris of the eye?
The one who'll think of it as window glass
And, passive, let the things before it pass,
And be, each thing and he, a passerby.

You close the curtain, let the vision die.
Yet eyes were never meant for looking *through*,
But rather *with*. The one that looked was *you*.
The lowered lid will draw the dawning nigh.

The sibyl had a world that whirled within;
Beyond her will, she would a vision win.
Not hollow, not burnt out, her citadel.
Enchanter-spirit, casting ample spell,
Surrounded she, as in Ezekiel
The Lord by angel-forms to Him akin.

(88) Fall of Absalom

They lifted them, swift, to noblesse:
The storm from the horn-call swelling
The silken, widely welling
Banners; of radiance telling,
The tent where he placed them, compelling,
The folk-jubilation not quelling,
Ten women to possess,

Who (used to the old one, at first,
King sparing in nightly deed)
Below approaching thirst
Waved as the summer seed.

And then he came out for advice,
Diminished not at all,
And those who beheld, in a trice,
Felt blinding light down fall.

Next he'd the army prepare,
Advance like the star of the year;
Over every spear
Wafted his warmer hair,
That free of his helmet would burst,
And which at times he'd hate,
Because it felt heavier there
Than his garments richly great.

An order gave the king
That handsome man to spare.

But reft of helmeting
One saw him in perilous place
Grim thugs in red chunks efface:
The soldier down he'd tear.
He vanished awhile from sight,
Until in a sudden affright
A cry: "He's hanging there,
On the terebinth bough, in the air,
With eyebrows pulled up tight!"

That signal was enough.
Joab, hunter rough,
Spied slanted branch where hung
The man, the trees among:
Ran through the suppliant slim,
Spear-bearers following him,
Slashing to left and to right.

(88) Reply

The king was grieved and moved and went
Up to the chamber over the gate
And wept, and as he went he said:
Would God that I had died for thee,
  O Absalom, my son, my son!

The boy whom God to David sent,
Gracious to one that loved him, elate,
Blest love had never forfeited
Though men he led in treachery.
  O Absalom, my son, my son!

What rarer jewel can be lent?
Children are humans' higher estate:
True love upsprung; hymns heav'nward sped;
In child's bright eye, we sky may see.
  O Absalom, my son, my son!

With highest minding, heaven meant
Father and son great praise would await.
From branch was hung the handsome head
When love was paid with tragedy.
  O Absalom, my son, my son!

(89) Esther

The servant maidens combed for seven days
The ashes that their sorrow-plague would raise,
The overthrow, abjection, from their hair;
They bore it, and they sunned it in the air
And added aromatic spices rare
This day and that, as they might best prepare.

The time was now at hand when she, unasked,
Without delay, and feeling as if dead,
To see the palace of her dread was tasked,
In order, leaning on her helpers dear,
At pathway's end to glimpse the one ahead,
Who loved one's death will threaten, drawing near.

The shine so bright!—she felt the rubies red
Flare up in fire upon the crown she wore;
With fit demeanor filled, she then was led
As royal vessel that would overpour

With plentitude of his monarchic might
Before she'd crossed the third high room of green,
That with its tall-built walls of malachite
Shone down upon her. She had not foreseen

So long a walk to make with precious stone
Far heavier in royal presence grown.
She went and went, by chilling fear made cold,

And as at last she viewed him almost near,
At ease upon his throne of tourmaline,
And towering, a giant object old,

She, fainting, with the right-hand servant's aid
To reach the throne the bravest effort made.
He touched her with the scepter-tip, and she—
She grasped it, feeling empty inwardly.

(89) Reply: Nikolay Gumilev's "Memory"

It is noon. With her quietened eyes
(Sparks are dancing, the sun-heat is throbbing)
Frightened bird in captivity cries.
Facing fate, she is silently sobbing.

She was lured by a subtle green snare,
And her eyes were enwrapped in a cover:
Blinding fog—she no longer could bear
To do more than keep flying, glide, hover ...

While the whirlwinds, capricious, lead on,
Unresponding to prayer, resistless—
From the earth now forever are gone
Pallid wings of the bird, limp and listless.

And whenever I see your sad gaze
Where restrained summer lightnings are hiding,
I recall the mute bird in her maze,
In her martyrdom, silently chiding.

(90) The Leper King

The leprosy arose upon his brow
And suddenly was there, below the crown,
Him as the king of horror to avow,
Who made them stare, the baffled and cast down,

This fearful happening to see complete
In one who seemed laced up, he was so thin,
To wait for one inquiring after him;
Yet none was man enough the test to meet:
It made him ever more untouched within—
This dignity and worth that would accrete.

(90) Reply

The boils of Job are those we don't deserve;
They teach no moral and they nothing serve.
He may be pardoned who will these bewail,
Though lamentation nothing can avail.

What is, remains; we, frail, are moved by mood.
The leap must infinite considered be
That reached from utter nothing unto me.
The war the principle of plenitude
Must make on nothing mind will have endued
With calm and luck if yet in grief I see,
Through all the nothing, that infinity.

(91) Legend of Three Living and Three Dead

They'd sported with falcons, the gentlemen three,
Then took in a tavern their ease.
But a graybeard the trio would seize—
Led them off! They could scarce bear to see
Three sarcophagi which, in the breeze

Were affecting them badly with triplicate stink,
In the mouth, in the nose, in the eyes;
And they knew right away: longer time than you'd
     think
The three dead ones had lain on the way to the
     brink,
And they'd wander, a horrid surprise.

And their hunter-hearing they'd yet kept high
And clear next the helmet-guard;
And the old one twitched his, hard:
But they never would go through the needle eye,
And from heaven they'd ever be barred.

And the senses were clear that their world enclasped,
Still strong from the hunting, and hot;
Yet a frost from behind had their bodies grasped,
And an ice-cold sweat was their lot.

(91) Reply

The needle-eye as metaphor
Of never-entered heaven door
Is richly sourced in scripture lore.

It's Biblical, Qur'anic, too.
Let's add another double view:
Flaubert and Baudelaire will do.

In *Malte Laurids Brigge* we
Are introduced to leprosy:
A beggar, ill—and kissed, pardee,

By Julian the Hospítaler,
The hero whom Flaubert'd prefer:
For him the loathsome fragrant were.

And "A Cadaver" Brigge praised,
A corpse to art-awareness raised
When Charles had "painted" it unfazed.

(92) The King of Münster

The royal hair was clipped:
The crown had downward slipped.
It bent, a bit, the ears,
Through which the monarch hears

A noisy hateful storm
(Mouths starved throughout the land).
He sat, to keep it warm,
Upon his cold right hand,

As sober as a poker.
The king was feeling sad:
His manhood, mediocre,
Was lax, the bed gone bad.

(92) Reply

Three hunters met their doubles
Who'd yet abide, though dead,
And had their future troubles
Well clarified, ahead.

The king's unlovely spouse
Will serve as double, too;
The ills whereof she'd grouse
Are heard, and brought to view.

Your double is the part
Your jekyll wants to hyde:
You'd better take to heart
The lesson s/he'll provide.

(93) Dance of Death

A dance, but no orchestra needed;
They hear in themselves a howl
As if each were a nest for an owl.
Their terror is wet as a boil,
And the pre-smell of rotting and spoil
For them is of odors the best.

They press on the dancer unheeded:
He's the one whose ribs have receded,
The gallant who best has completed
The perfect dancing pair.
And he waves a cloth for the nun
To look at, over her hair;
They dance with their equals there.
Her face wax-pale in his wake,
The bookmark away he'll take
From her Book of Hours, for fun.

Now everyone's getting too hot,
For their garments are much too rich;
A sweating, acidic, will itch
Brows, buttocks, like as not,
And damage hat, mantle and jewel;
They're wishing they naked were
As a child, mind-united, a fool—
Yet a steady beat prefer.

(93) Reply: Alexander Pushkin's untitled verses from "Feast in Time of Plague"

When wilding winter in her might,
As valiant captain, leads the fight,
The shagged militia troops are snows
And storm and frost by night and day.
But crackling hearth can cold oppose,
With wintry heat the feast made gay.

The queen of threat, in scoffer crown,
The plague herself to us comes down:
Appealing, heaped-up harvest great!
Through thinnest window day and night—
What now? What aid?—we see our fate,
We hear the graveyard spade in fright.

As from the winter's cruel play,
From plague let's lock ourselves away:
We'll light the fire, the goblet fill,
All heedlessly to drown our thought,
At banquets and in ballrooms mill,
To laud the plague queen as we ought.

There is a drunkenness in fight,
In prospect of the pit of night,
In wilding waves of ocean main,
In blackened waters' storm-roar vague,
In the Arabian hurricane,
And in the panting of the plague.

Whatever sends the threat of death
Will hold for mortal heart and breath
Delights we cannot comprehend—
Perchance a pledge of deathless life;
That man is lucky who'll contend
To find and know them, bold in strife.

And so, to you, O plague, all praise!
Unfazed we face the end of days,
Hear unappalled your call of death.
We foam the goblets up: they're filled!
Drink, friendly, of the rose-maid breath
That's maybe with the plague instilled.

(94) The Last Judgment

Frightened with a fear entirely new,
Void of order, often wounded, loose,
Burst from field-clay of an ochre hue,
Feeling shrouds to comfort still conduce

(Thus are they conditioned to what fits),
Bearing oil, they note, the angels hie
Which they'll drop in body-sockets dry,
'Neath a person's arms to rub in pits

What within a life that efforts tried
Had not ever been desanctified;
Adding warmth to places withered, old,

So the hand of God would not get cold
Touching them, above, from every side,
Soft, the life to test, if 'twould abide.

(94) Reply

I'll likely lose my link to ochred clay
And to the shroud I wore where I was laid.
But need I spend my realm-of-heaven day
In death-time body, ill and weary made?

For resurrection of the flesh I prayed
And now am grateful, more than I can say.
But, too, my teeth have rotted quite away.
And then, my wounded leg, the saber-flayed,

Replaced with walking stick, was part repaid
With honor tribute later in parade
But made me, crippled, limp. Since undismayed

I bore my loss, may I implore Your aid
To get the old (the young) one back? I stayed
Your faithful laborer, and unafraid.

(95) The Temptation

Spike and thorn provide no spirit-gains
When they're thrust into the lusty flesh;
Bending senses threw, with labor pains,
Graveyard wails, and cries that wildly mesh:

Early births abortive, crooked-leering
Crawling, raving, crazy-flying creatures,
Nothings, anger-pitching imps appearing,
Grim alliance bound, with teasing features.

These in turn a generation bore,
For the pack were fruitful in the night
And when scattered in a motley war
Monsters multiplied beyond his sight.
From the whole a horrid drink was made,
Vessel-handle for his hands to take,
And a haunch, a thigh the nearest shade
Shoving, warm, would to embrace awake—.

Now he shouted to the angel, cried:
And the angel did in radiance come.
There he was—yet back inside
Demons reinclosed the holy one,

So that he with beast and demon-leer
Would contend as many years before,
And the God, the never-yet-made-clear,
From the férment would distill, outpour.

(95) Reply

Anthony appears to have become—
May we say?—a Reformation saint.
Gaze within to seek your halidom;
Spurn the outward devils that they paint.

See? it grows within, the demon-beast.
Look into your heart, and read, and write.
Pose not any query to a priest;
Pat, the answer you would thus invite.

If you'd rather craft an art Romantic,
You a scripture can yourself indite.
Mephistopheles and Faust alight
On the spirit map where, avid, antic,
They for sixty years or more will fight.
Demons you'll encounter, frenzied, frantic,
Heaven-manic angels corybantic:
Still within will be their source of might.

From within, your scriptor-impulse take.
Face the demon with the inner eye:
You may find, disguised, a brother nigh.
Loving, to the consequences wake.

What the folk provided isn't fake:
Thor is warring; shaking Phoebus-rays
Show Elias' windy flaming plays.
Luther leads to Goethe leads to Blake.

(96) The Alchemist

The vessel—calm, half-smoking—smilingly
The lab technician pushed away, refusing.
He now knew what he should, should not, be using
To make that lofty object come to be

That he was making. Ages he would need,
Millennia, for that alembic-pear
To brew; he must on constellations feed
In brain and, too, must have the ocean there.

The thing enormous that he'd hoped to hold—
He let it loose that night. Might it return
To God, its former scale to have, as best!

But he, still babbling more than drunkard bold,
Bent over secret lore, and yet would burn
With love for that one gold-crumb he possessed.

(96) Reply

The alchemist who knows he won't contain
The constellations and the ocean main
Within the mind that's trying to conceive
Philosophorum lapidem his brain

Will need to empty of ambition vain,
And, even if it may occasion pain,
Dismiss the phantoms that he can't believe.
For only so will come the spirit-gain.

The theories are gone, yet he the grain
Of gold desires. Then ought the reader grieve
To think that greed can still for years remain?

Ah, no. *Malorum radix* may not wane,
Yet man desireless? Mean, unbreathing bane.
To live, our want with dream we interweave.

(97) The Reliquary

Those outside are waiting for the rings,
Every part of the prophetic chain
Telling fates it aided to occur;
Inside only were the things, the things
That he forged; before the smith there were
None but crown alone: he'd bend and frame
Just that thing alone, a trembling one,
Which he'd, darkly as in anger, train
For the bearing of a perfect stone.

Steadily his eyes were getting colder
From the daily and the chilly drink;
Finally the splendid finished holder
(Costly beaten gold, high-carated)
Stood complete before him, votive link,
Gift, oblation: might a little wrist
Find it—white, well-shaped and wizarded:

Endlessly on bended knee he stayed,
Weeping and abandoned, no more daring,
Soul subjecting, nothing caring:
Ruby in her peace arrayed
Seemed aware of him and made
Inquiry about his being—staring,
Him from dynasties surveyed.

(97) Reply

Emblemed femininity, the rose;
Tulip, charcoal remnant at the base,
Calyx-image of the burnt-out case:
Tired the fire that climbed, the eyes that close.
Rose and tulip ardent fates enlace.
Too, the ruby in the cup of wine
Is a fire that would the dying king
Old in Thulë to remembrance bring:
Goblet gone when lives no more entwine!

Tulip, rose, and ruby: fire design.
Flames that bright disciple-brow would crown
Now in rhodal glory-gaze refine
One who, guided by a Lady's face,
Warmed in splendor of celestial eyne,
Bowed his head, on cloudlets looking down,
Overpowered by the sacred place.

Lord of Daybreak, may our flames align
Aim and striving; ruby wine of grace,
Kind, alembicate for those who race
Pardon to receive and for a sign
Mindful are that, after sunrays drown,
Ocean sunken shining will unclose
When her henna'd palm the dawn-maid shows.

(98) Gold

What if it were not: it would have had
Finally in mountains born to be,
Then be tossed away to rivers, free,
By the will, the fermentation glad

Of their will, their theme obsessively,
That one ore excels the other ores.
Widely threw they out what heart outpours
Ever more from Meroë

To the bound of lands, ethereal sky,
Over all experience to roam;
And the sons would bring it with a sigh—
What the fathers promised would be nigh,
Hardened, devastated, to their home

Where it stayed a certain time and grew,
Leaving then the ones it weakened, who
Never felt it to endear.
Now (they say), the recent long nights through,
It, arisen, views them clear.

(98) Reply

Gold is brilliant, and the Lord is light,
Milton wrote, and theologians taught.
Yet we store it all in vaults of night,
In economy-enigma caught.

Gold, the source of glory and of sorrow,
Seemed the seed of light divinely sown;
From the sun a shine it seemed to borrow.
Tempted, though, Cortés and then Pizarro,
Paragon deceivers having grown,
Captured lands would ravish; their intention
Was: when foreign kings were overthrown
All the gold, through godly intervention,
Would be granted to the Spanish Throne.

Gold's interpreted in alchemy
As an emblem of eternity.
Yet it's often ominously red;
So for this would many murdered be:
Shining idol-calf, ensanguined head.

(99) The Stylite

Folk who judged him would to battle come,
Whom he'd send to hell or halidom.
Realizing he was lost, thought daft,
Over folk-repute he climbed with numb
Hands up high upon a column shaft,

Never halting till he reached the height
And upon the level platform stays
Now, comparing well, to get them right,
His debility, his Savior's praise;

Never ending, this: he yet compared;
Ever greater did the Other seem.
And the farmer, shepherd, raftsman stared;
Saw him small, beside himself, in dream

Speaking always with the sky entire,
Sometimes rained on, other times in light;
And upon them plunged his howling dire—
Howling in your face, in high despite!
Years, below, was hidden from his sight

How the crowd's great pressure, energy,
More complete became, and more fulfilled.
Prince-bedizenment no more instilled
Former glory, rising free.

But when he above, near-damned, denied,
Torn apart by their opposing force,

Lonely, with a desperation-cry,
Demons wrathful shook away, threw down,
What would fall at first from site on high
Heavy, awkward, from the wounds of course,
Were the worms that in each open crown
Landed, and on velvet multiplied.

(99) Reply

Witty Rilke, sly, unorthodox,
Loves a punchline anecdote to craft
That complacent expectation mocks.
Many are the times I've shouted, laughed;
White the water on our hazard-raft.
Simeon Stylites I had met:
But the Tennyson soliloquy,
Seeming too predictable to me,
Meant the reader'd never lose the bet.

Monster of a solitary pride,
Simple Simeon on pillar stayed:
Anglican, the Laureate defied
Catholic salvation so portrayed.

Easy to deride the obsolete,
Styles of piety to feel as fleet,
Passing ways of cultivating passion,
Praising rather modern skeptic fashion:
Laud Today, and they'd applaud, how sweet.

If we let the poet switch the terms
Into spirit-will, not deadened letter,
Moral lessons issue from the worms,
And the birthing wounds are smelling better.
So originality affirms
Generosity the heav'n begetter.
Trend-abettor or a form-upsetter,
Moral allegory spurns or sperms.

(100) Mary of Egypt

Since the time when, hot from bed, as whore
Over Jordan gone, as if a grave
Off'ring, yet empowered all the more,
Drink eternal, pure, her heart she gave

Grew an early deep fidelity,
Unrestrainable, to such a height
That she finally, as turned to light
Essence, body yellowed ivory,

Lay in husk of long and brittle hair.
Lion circled; sage came into view,
Called him, nodding; aid he needed there
(And they buried her, these two)

And the old one put her in, alone.
Lion, like a man who'd scutcheon bear,
Stood nearby and held the stone.

(100) Reply

Makários, a man of calm demeanor,
Known for absolving flaws in fellow beings,
Viewing a thief onto a beast of burden
Loading the holy father's own possessions,

Helped him complete the task and, spirit tranquil,
Bade him farewell. When questioned, he would
     counsel:
"Timothy said it best: 'We came with nothing
Into the world,' and further: 'It is certain

We carry nothing out.'" A pupil queried:
"What is the fit and proper mode of prayer?"
"Extend your hands," he showed, "While saying only:
'Lord, as you will; and as you know, have mercy.'"

(101) Crucifixion

Used to dragging to the hanging-place
Any kind of riff-raff, rabble gang,
They would let the heavy menials hang,
Turned from time to time a twisted face

Toward the three they'd been disposing of.
For the executioners, above,
Though, an ill occurred; the job complete,
Men attending, shambling, shuffled feet.

One (meat-curer faced, with spots of tan)
Cried: "That man—he shouted out some word!"
And the mounted leader asked, "Which man?"
For it seemed to him he too had heard,

Loud, Elijah's name invoked. And all
Got excited, eager now to see,
And they offered, putting off his fall,
Curious, the vinegar and gall,
While he coughed, yet faintingly.

They had hoped for a dramatic play
(Might Elijah, too, be stopping by?)
But, behind, heard Mary's distant cry:
Then he roared and fell away.

(101) Reply

Eli, Eli! means *My God, My God!*
That is what the stunned official heard
Though he failed to comprehend the word.
Irony intentional, not odd:

We may claim it hadn't been an error;
For Elijah served as emblem-sign
Of another herald high, divine,
Jesus' John the Baptist; thus the terror
Which had filled a killer's heart can be
Allegorically understood:

Nailed upon the crucifixion-wood,
Why, my God, have You forsaken me?
Christ had cried, in bleak humility.
Well may we recall the voice of one
Crying in the wilderness in pain.
Sufferer-Elijah, like the Son,
Thought his life and mission all in vain,

Yet would hear, within, the quiet voice
Which at length would consolation lend.
Jesus, when he faced the fatal end,
Likewise heard the final word: *Rejoice.*

(102) The Resurrected One

He was able even to the end
To refuse to her or to deny
That her love should celebrated be;
Sank she at the cross on bended knee
In the garb of pain, beleaguered by
Stones they cast, she yet would love her Friend.

But on coming to apply the salve,
At the tomb she stood, where tears would flow,
He arose, more holiness to have
For her higher weal when saying, No—

In her hollow, she had heard Him right:
He, by death empowered, unafraid,
Pleasure of the oil that makes one light
And her early feelings now forbade

That He might, of her, a lover form
Who'd no more to one she loved incline;
She, though, torn by an enormous storm,
Overrode that voice divine.

(102) Reply

Gospel writers three asseverate:
Mary Magdalen had been the first
Who the Christ, new-risen and elate,
Viewed when He the tomb had burst.
She by judges harsh had been accurst:
Now behold her grown in spirit great.

Some have thought Messiah meant to show
Passion's never meant to be despised
When the seeker will have realized
Where the God-directed love must go.

One who wrote her gospel disagreed;
Here she conquered seven forms of wrath:
Darkness, ignorance, and zeal for death,
Flesh, desire, flesh-wisdom and its realm,
Transient anger. Gnostic leader, she.

She's become a penitent indeed,
Earth denier on the upward path,
Seeking bliss that ever sévereth
Heav'n from world, Sophia at the helm,
So achieving endless liberty.

(103) Magnificat

Already heavy, on the slope she rose,
Near-skeptical of hope and faith and aid;
But when the tall, supporting matron made
An earnest, proud attempt to help (she knows,

Thought Mary, all; there's nothing left to tell),
She suddenly felt calm, breathed tranquilly;
The cautious women, grave, conducted well,
Would wait for her to speak: "It feels to me

As if I, now and evermore, were love.
God from the wealthy idle shakes away
The shine, that we will now see nothing of.
Yet seeks He out one woman, from above,
Fills her with distant time, with what will stay.

He found me, then. Consider, tidings roll,
For me, from star to star from Him adored.

Exalt and glorify, my joyful soul,
As high as you can cry, the LORD."

(103) Reply

When Mary in her chamber stayed alone,
Her guardian was startled to discern
An angel, to her hidden alcove shown,
To her with nourishment to turn.

And when the blessed time was drawing near,
She lay beneath a desert date-palm tree.
Her labor pains were great, yet she would see
Inclining branches furnish fruit and cheer.

A stream, with water freshening and sweet,
A wonder-thing, appearing near her feet,
More sustenance would grant, to let her rest
In calm until the baby would appear.
With gratitude she waked, her son to greet,
And thanked the Lord of Daybreak, Holiest.

Messiah, Word of God, would Jesus be,
So may we in Islamic writing see:
What I have told of Mary and this man
I borrowed from the volume named Qur'an.

(104) Adam

On the steep cathedral stair, amazed,
Adam stands, beholding window-roses,
Nearly scared by the apotheosis
That had grown and so respect had raised;

Over this one, over that he's placed;
Towering, he likes the life he spent
Plainly framed: the farmer first who went,
All beginning, nothing knowing, faced,

Leaving the completed Eden fair,
Not by any highway out of there.
God, the unpersuadable, stood by,

Who would threaten, never quite aware
Of the steady fact that he would die.
Humans, though, would last, would live, would bear.

(104) Reply

Laud it, for we hear it with relief:
Long we've read of fall and fear and grief.
Time to reassess the Adam-blessing;
Likely you'll agree with me, I'm guessing.

Firstness will itself encourage; we,
Adam-glad, enjoy priority.
Next, determination we admire:
Boldly to pursue a new desire.

Then, invention and resourceful strength
Greatly lessened the remorse, at length:
Garden-man a farmer soon will be.

Lastly, fruitfulness, fertility.
Wise men teach: Who cannot add subtracts.
Death divides, but Adam interacts.

(105) Eve

Simply standing on cathedral stair,
Near the splendor of the window-rose,
With the apple in the apple-pose,
Guiltless-guilty aye, as painted there,

For the growing one whom she would bear
Since the circle of eternities
Leaving, loving; wandering, she sees
All the world, a striding springtime-fair.

Ah, she would have gladly on that ground
Been allowed to stay, and there to see
Creatures' understanding, harmony.

But her man she resolute had found;
Him, one eye on death, she joined, and she
Scarcely knew as yet of deity.

(105) Reply

Here, as in the Adam picture, I
Find some liking for the Wisdom Tree:
Modified, the grim disparity
That would show our life as but a sigh.

Eve no longer is informed that she
Progeny must bear, her painful cry
Lasting penalty, nor must deny
Honor, serving Adam-mastery.

There's a wary, quiet prophecy
Hidden in the final line, pardee:
Mary to her Lord will come more nigh.

Eve herself, though, is a vernal Tree
Of the Life which yet would come to be
Through the Lady livened by the sky.

(106) Uncertain in the Garden

Dijon

Still shut is the Carthusian House, retired,
The wall-surrounded court secure and healed;
A pause the ones that live within desired,
Denying life outside, for one revealed;

Whatever might have come, gone safely by.
They gladly walk on their accustomed ways,
Withdrawing, meeting, as in ancient days,
So primal circling will within would lie.

True, many cultivate the springtime beds;
In meekness, neediness, they, quiet, kneel;
And no one sees what they within can feel:
A something secret, dizzied in their heads,

A gesture for the early tender grass,
A testing, wary, and reserved caress:
For green's a friend, but roses' red duress
May be a threat and an excess, alas,

And, too, perhaps again will overrise
That which the soul can recognize and knows.
But this, abiding silent, will be wise;
How kind the grass that gently grows!

(106) Reply

The grass, how humble: it will never balk
When by however many trod upon.
In freshened strength bejeweled, by the dawn
Bedewed and ready for the next that walk.

It lacks the blatant red of manly yang,
And, too, the lady-folds ensouled with yin;
Not virile, nor appearing feminine.
It springs today as in the past it sprang.

Who bow before the Lord are like the grass:
They prostrate fall before the holy feet
By which was evening Eden trodden, sweet;
They hail the God of hope, for woe shall pass.

I, a survivolinist, would belaud
The one to rise and fall and rise again,
By wind bestrummed, and in the summer rain:
The grassblade, by the sun in homage awed.

I hymn the grass, and raise my glass to Him
By Whom, made green and wise, may life endure:
The breath of them is jubilant and pure
With gift of its invigorating vim.

(107) The Puzzled Ones

And they're silent; the partition walls
In their mind no longer stay;
Hours, unless their understanding falls,
Lifted up and gone away.

Night: they'll often draw to window near:
All is good, so suddenly.
On a thing concrete their hands they lay,
And the heart is high, and they can pray,
Eyes are gazing in tranquillity—

Often twisted seemed this unhoped thing:
Garden, rest-contented in the square,
That in alien worlds' light-mirroring
Grows and never vanishes from there.

(107) Reply

They are growing up: wild wonder-thing.
Thus had Eve, past Eden, waking world
Seen as at her feet the spring unfurled.
Walls are gone; a psalm we sing.

Garden? It was guarded, and enwalled,
Wisdom a forbidden Tree.
Unexamined life? That's not for me.
Pall of death has left us unappalled:
Virgo, vir sunt *virga, vita, vis*—

Virgin, man, staff, life, and *strength* in this!
Being, so enhanced, will burst in bloom.
Filled with angels, mind has twofold room:
Eden-freed, we gain: O rain of bliss!

(108) From the Life of a Saint

Came anguished fears. Of these the entering
Had been like death, could not be overcome.
His heart had learned to go through slowly: bring
It up—so he would try, as if a son.

And then of nameless needs he came to know,
Each dark, with no tomorrow, like a blow;
The soul he next gave up, wise follower,
When she was grown, as it were best for her

To lie beside the Bridegroom, Lord. He stayed
Behind, alone, would in a place remain
Where solitude all other goods outweighed:
He lived remote, from words could nothing gain.

Yet, after time gone by, there came to view
A happiness delivered to his hand
So that a tenderness he'd understand
In lying quiet as the creatures do.

(108) Reply

The heart and soul a son and daughter! He
Must give the children over to the One.
He gave them up, he breathed them out, begun
A selfless being, lending liberty.

Cloud of Unknowing tells the world that we
Dividually feel a malison,
A melancholy. Whom it cannot stun
To be a severed self needs pitied be.

The holy one his heart, soul, outward sighs,
Remaining silence, never want of word.
Creaturely being, though, in compromise

Came as a lightening, a dow'r deferred.
He feels that he, like bird and cloud and star,
Is God-beloved—ev'n from Him afar.

(109) The Beggars

You haven't grasped what I'm telling
Of the crowd. A strange gaze lands
On beggars there, who are selling
The hollows of their hands.

They show the one who'll arrive
A mouth that's filled with dung,
And he'll see (if he has the drive)
How leprosy eats the tongue.

His face in their devastated
Gaze melts away, as fit:
They've seduced him, and they are elated,
And when he speaks, they spit.

(109) Reply: Nikolay Gumilev's "Sly Devil"

My devil, best of merrymakers,
A song had made, and cleverly:
"All night the sailor breasted breakers,
Dawn saw him deep beneath the sea."

Ascended wave-walls, taller, vaunted,
Then fell, then foamed and rose again.
More white than foam he saw, undaunted,
His love, above the ocean plain.

He struggled on, he heard her calling—
'I love you, dear, as you love me'—
"But," said the devil, "kept on falling.
Dawn saw him deep beneath the sea."

(110) Foreign Family

Much as the dust that started who knows where
And then was nowhere, with no aim explained
Shows in a corner (empty morning air!)—
One sees the gray is growing that remained—

So had they seen themselves, and who knows why,
The final moment, right before your tread;
They were a thing uncertain, waiting by,
Amid low spirits of the lane-life dead

That longed for you. Or maybe not for you;
For then a voice, as coming from last year,
To you was singing, yet seemed weeping more;
And then a hand, that borrowed seemed though
          true,
Extended, never grasped your hand so dear.
Who'll come then, yet? What do they hope, these
          four?

(110) Reply

We cannot help but see the shapes in blue
Appearing to convey a grief unnamed,
Their faces of an enervated hue,
As if awaiting something, or ashamed,

Or fated, in a season of decline,
To wander, or in spirit waste away,
Although the cause of anguish to divine
We're at a loss, and speculating stray

In reverie about a waning age.
A circus worker, acrobat, who tries
In motley costume vainly to disguise
A woe unknown to me: the dreamer mage
Picasso had imprinted on the mind
Ennui of those who seek and cannot find.

(111) Corpse Washing

They'd got accustomed to him, yes. But when
The kitchen lamp came in and, restless, burned
(Dark draft), the one of whom they'd nothing learned
Was unknown, wholly. They his neck washed then,

And since they nothing knew about his fate,
They put together something in the mind
And washed some more. A cough, a little wait,
Then one a sponge with vinegar would find

To put upon his face. A pause at first:
The other stopped. From hard and close-cut hair
The droplets plopped; cramped hand (the eye 'twould
        scare
To look) would make the viewers twain aware
He nevermore within this world would thirst.

He made that clear enough. To work they set
As if embarrassed, faster (cough again);
The curving shadow on the carpet let
A flowing form be intertwined with them,

The mute designs, a skein, a single net,
Until the washing come to final pause.
Through window glass, uncurtained, would descend
The night, relentless—enter to contend;
Bare, pure, he lay, the nameless, giving laws.

(111) Reply

In *Malte Laurids Brigge* manifold
Is death; *hi termini mortalium,*
Distinct in individuated gloom,
With patience, and in great detail, are told.

The moment, though, that vividest to me
Appeared, and now comes back, was never called
A death, yet oh! the panic that appalled
The fevered boy who far too much could see ...

Delirium had pictures brought, and deeds,
Adventures, fact and fancy, overload
Of self in overflow: he couldn't goad
The spirits hovering; none hearing heeds.
Then came the rage: the heap of demons grew,
But youth would prove their equal, and would do
Almighty feats of will to drive them to
Be centered in the self again, squeezed in,
Shut down! No strength was given him to win
The fight. He lay, *all open,* while they flew:
He panicked, yelled, and yelled into the air—
Fell back. Saw shadows, and a candle flare.

(112) One of the Old Women

Paris

Sometimes (do you know how it can be?)
In the evening suddenly they'll stand,
Sideways nod: a smile, in patches and
Under halfway hidden hat we see.

Then a building will appear beside,
Endless, and along it they invite
With the riddle of their scabby blight,
With the cape, hat, corridor not wide;

And the hand behind the collar stays
That is waiting and that longs for you;
Clasp your hands, that's what it wants to do,
Which around the paper still you raise.

(112) Reply

Film technique: the shadows from the hat
And the building and the evening dusk
Let the smile in patches gleam; a musk
Hints alluring mood in wind, like that.

Next the wall is partly lighted, so
Outlines brighten of the hat and cape,
While a passageway reveals a shape
And an injured face a past will show.

Finally the gleam will focus on,
First, her hand, and then the both of his;
Étude themed in light and dark, it is:
Black and gray and bright and dim and wan.

(113) The Blind Man

Paris

Look, he goes, and interrupts the town;
It cannot occupy his darkened place
That, darker crack, will brighter cup deface.
As on a leaf is painted and set down,

For him, the dim-reflected form of things—
Alas, not taken in, a thing of naught.
Alone his feeling's touched, as if it caught
A world in little waves and rippled rings:

A quietness, and an opposing stand.
Now: whom to choose? He, wondering, will tarry.
Devotedly he'll raise a giving hand,
In nearly festive way, as if to marry.

(113) Reply: Charles Baudelaire's "The Blind"

Consider these, my friends: they're really an affright!
Vague-ludicrous, the look the mannequins yet keep:
As, terrible, unique, they seem to walk in sleep,
Their darkened globes will dart—but where?—into
    the night.

Their eyes, from which the spark divine is lost and
      gone,
As if they gazed from far away, remaining raised
To heaven, never look at pavement: still unfazed,
They will not dream with heavy head, bent down and
    wan.

And so they cross the dark that limit none will find—
The dark, eternal silence' brother. City! While,
Around, your chant, laugh, bellow sound and
    interwind,

With pleasures smit that to atrocity beguile,
I drag myself about, more dazed than they my smile:
What are they seeking in their heaven, all these
    blind?

(114) A Weazened Woman

Lightly, as after its death,
She carries the cloth, the glove:
From her dresser drawer, a breath
Strove with aroma she'd love

Where, before, she could recognize
Herself. Now she asks not who
She is (distant relative sighs):
She wanders, while thoughts pursue ...

She looks for a worrisome room
Which can arrange her, and spare,
For yet always—may she assume?—
The same girl's living there.

(114) Reply

The favored theme of Proust:
The fragrance of time elapsed.
A remembered aroma loosed
Can hold us anew, enclasped.

Unsevered, layered me's
In senses are coded yet
Where a smell a self can seize
And in resurrection set.

The I in whom I believe
Is of many lost ones made,
And the thief who will bereave
May himself be weazened, fade.

(115) Evening Meal

Toward us urges the eternal. Who
Can choose the big, small pow'rs to separate?
You daily see through dusk of trade-days late
The evening meal in rear-placed room ensue:

How they behave, how they extend things to
Each other; simple, heavy-slow, at rest.
And from a hand a sign will rise, a test;
They know not how it happens, what they do

While ever speaking certain words anew
When placing what we drink and what we share.
But there is none who journeys won't accrue,
Who won't in secret leave, delaying there.

And is there not among them always one
Who'll send his parents, though they serve and care,
Away when all their helpful time is done?
(To sell them?—no, indeed; he wouldn't dare.)

(115) Reply

Well, here I felt the shock a second time.
And *Malte Laurids Brigge* was the first.
The prose account is echoed in the rhyme:
The Spendthrift Son had prayed, with eager thirst,

That he might not be loved; a troubadour
Of longing, courtly lauding lore was he,
Resisting answerable earthly lure
And faithful to the Height: a Manichee.

Toward us urges the eternal. We,
In free unreachability immersed,
For Her are yearning, for eternity,
For what will draw us on, epluriversed.

Ingratitude is not a sin or crime,
Though cynical it seem. It is a pure
Attraction past the transient. The sublime
Names tragic only what may soul immure.

(116) Site of a Fire

Mistrustfully evaded by the morn
Of early fall, beneath the linden trees
That, singed, the heath-house crowded, now one sees
An emptiness, a playing-place new-born:

Children, from who knows where, shout merrily
To one another; rags they try to snatch.
They suddenly were quiet, though, when he,
The son, to forking branch would next attach

A kettle, ashy woodbeams, curving trough,
In order that, as if he told a lie,
He, looking down, might all the children spy
For whom the spectacle he'd carry off:

Look what was here! They'd know, they'd understand.
For since it all was gone, to him it seemed
Fantastical as Pharaoh, something dreamed,
And he was—other. From an alien land.

(116) Reply

I'm dreaming, too: the pharaoh seems the key;
The fire that struck the nearby home, a plague.
The parallel's enchantment, as a vague
And legendary venue comes to be.

A child's in love with magic: it defies
Bland habit and predictability.
Could Moses turn a rod to serpent? He
Was not alone, in learning not more wise

Than wielders of Egyptian magic art;
In wizardry, they're eager to compete:
The more the miracles, the greater treat.
And here's the principle that's at the heart

Of what diversified the plaguy plan:
Ten wonder-shows are ten times better than
A single stunt. Descending from the sky,
Divine affright delights the childish eye.

(117) The Group

Paris

As if one quickly plucked for a bouquet:
The faces are arranged by hasty chance;
One it moves back, or might again advance,
Grabs three in back, a near one puts away,

Or switches this and that, promotes one, fresh,
Rejects, like weed, a dog that wouldn't mesh;
A plant that's bowed and bore a humble brunt
It moves, through leaves and stalks, up to the front

And binds it, tiny, leaning on the brim;
Then, reaching back, will change, replace, collate;
And now has time a better view to win

By leaping back: positioned on the mat,
One moment more—the smoothened form, the weight
Wielder is heavy-swelled and looking fat.

(117) Reply

Gewichteschwinger, wielder of the weights,
What randomness—of all their fragile fates
Of whom the faces, humble as the grass,
We feel, may fall; things come to be, they pass.

The artist of a world occasions fright:
They serve a strange aesthetic will-to-might
Whose lives are written in the book of light
And darkness that photo-graphy is hight.

Er *seine Schwere schwellt*: while heaviness
With child, with art, is great, their fates are less.
The demi-urge, if only half a god,

Has arbitrary will for staff and rod.
The "for itself" became an "in itself,"
Thing-object made in mind of impish elf.

(118) Snake Charmer

If swaying conjurer in market-square
May pipe on flute of gourd, that charms and lulls,
It might occur: a hearer's lured and mulls
Upon what's heard, from stalls surrounding there

In tumult drawn, encircled by the flute,
That wants and wants and wants and that assures
The basket-reptile stiffen—air that lures,
The stiffened making languid, tune astute

To alternate, in fainting way and blind,
That which will scare, extend; make loose and lax;
A look's enough, the Indian will find,
Who's poured in something strange that racks,

In which you're dying, as if fallen on
By glowing heaven. Then there spreads a crack
Across your face. Of spices now no lack
Laid on your northern memory, soon gone,

That cannot aid. No power you defends;
The sun ferménts; the fever victim lies;
Malicious glee the shaft a stiffness lends;
And venoms gleam in serpent eyes.

(118) Reply

Observe the rod of Dionysus here,
That altered thyrsus, lushly wine-enwound,
Twin theme of stiff and limp, might now appear
In new and melded emblem blent and crowned.

A hidden violence in luxuries,
A vigor in effeminacy clad,
So in the *Bacchae* of Euripides
A heady freedom may enchain the mad.

The heaven's tropical, and then it strikes;
The victim willed the ill that would entice.
The pinecone top, the spiteful thistle-spikes:
Will phoenix rearise from bed of spice?

(119) Black Cat

Spectre I would liken to a place
Where your image with a sound collides;
But, where waiting fur of black abides,
Something will your strength of gaze efface:

So a raving madman who, pell-mell,
Crazily into the black will stamp,
Quickly in compliant padded cell
Finds the rage abate, the ardor damp.

Every image that an impress makes,
She appears within herself to hide,
So that, menacing and sorely tried,
She will look, and next a nap she takes.
Then she'll quickly turn her face, awake,
Centered on the middle of your own,
And you'll meet your image, no mistake,
In the amber of each pupil-stone,
Wholly unawaited, locked inside
Like an insect, long extinct, that died.

(119) Reply

Something troubling in the distance of
(Royal and refined) the feline face
May arouse a doubt about the love
We may find, despite abundant grace.

Green or yellow gleams the limpid lake,
Yet a glassy mirror's all that we,
Notwithstanding tender care we take,
View, without a movement or a "me."

Even though Abu Huraira claimed
That the blessed Prophet truly said
Proper to the faith is love of cats,
Yet an ancient poet, unashamed,
Offered us a twin portrayal that's
Faithful to the ways the cat is "read."
"Soft as Bástet," gentle can it be;
"Wild as Sékhmet," too: contrarily,
Lifting up a fierce and eager head,
Like the lion-headed deity
She a vengeance might prepare instead.

(120) Before Easter

Naples

Through the high-curbed lanes that spread
Past the homes in towers laid,
Dark beneath to harbor-aim,
Gold will roll, of great parade;
Splendid quilts, inherited,
High, on balcony displayed,
(Each a greater height may claim)
Mirroring the flow, will aid.

Momently on door will knock
One abundantly supplied;
Products ever more they pull.
Strutting seem the selling-stands;
On the corner, men will hawk
Fresh-killed ox, and what's inside;
Crosswalk, banner bragging-full;
Myriad stores of varied stock

Load the benches, hang from pegs,
Pile, compel; from dusky gleam
Of the doors, before the yawn
Of the melons, types of bread.
Greedy, active, ev'n the dead;
Quieter the hens, and calm;
Goats that hang from ceiling beam;
Gentler lamb with outstretched legs

Borne by youth on shoulder here,
Nodding-headed to his walk,
While behind the walls the glazed
Spanish Mary clasps will show,
Diadems of silver clear,
Gleaming lights anticipating.
What is in the window waiting?
Spendthrift-eyed, an ape below
Who objections will have raised,
Making gestures: some will balk.

(120) Reply

Reader, I with gratitude
Your indulgence will receive,
Should it be in kindness given.
I have done a daring thing:
Choosing five-beat lines to sing
Using only four, I've striven
More compression to achieve,
By conciser frame endued.

Principle of plenitude!
That's the feeling I believe
Rilke's thinking here has driven:
Push and jostle, heave and swing,
Crushing, crowding, rush and fling—
So communities have thriven;
Lack will barely lives bereave
By festivities imbued.

Even if baboons are lewd,
Little need the proper grieve
Who their gravity may leaven
When the festive church-bells ring
And the banner's colored wing
Intimates the hues of heaven
Bright with red and blue at eve:
Rife is life with rough and rude.

(121) The Balcony

Naples

Narrowed by the balcony above,
Set in order, as with painter's love,
And arranged for festival bouquet
Of the oval and the aging faces,
These at eve, ideal in added graces,
We more touching find, and made for aye.

Two appear, upon each other leant:
Sisters, who, as if, when distanced, they
Wanly hoped they might together play,
Loneliness to loneliness, are bent;

And the brother, with the solemn air,
Silent, something shut, though still polite,
Yet by softened moment, unaware,
Made a mirror of his mother, quite;

And between, unlived, slow-heavy face,
Every link to relatives undone,
Grizzled woman's mask, approached by none,
As if grasped by hand and kept in place,

While a second one's more weazened, gray,
Gliding-minded, not intent to stay,
Lower, garment-framed, not far away

From the child-face, new-attempted, set
Well in order, rather faded, pale,
Striped with bars of iron from the rail,
Undetermined as a thing not-yet.

(121) Reply

Yes, he loved Cézanne and, too, a book
Wrote about Rodin, and even speaks
Of a painter, yet the mind that seeks
For the way that face-arranging look
Might have been acquired may want to see
Nearer sources in photography.

How a personality has grown
Quick, precise detailing may reveal.
In the post-impressionsts I've known
Swift or stylized features more conceal
Than of deep psychology they've shown.

Here's a photo studio supreme:
Sitters make their own arrangement-frame;
Faces, quietened, remain the same
Long enough to offer up a theme.

Unpredictably, a sudden shift
Equally may show the double-side
Of the Jekyll-face, or of the Hyde;
Watchers feel the spirit fall or lift.

Best, we view within the families
Linked-elusive personalities,
Each a random-wandered congeries.

I have had my charcoal portrait drawn.
First were many photo poses caught;
These were molded to a thing of thought
Later, when the subject home had gone.

(122) Ship of Émigrés

Think of it as one who, white-hot, fled,
With the victors left behind in vain;
Suddenly he made it plain
He was brave, and, turning back, would gain,
'Gainst the hundreds, payback for the pain:
Fruit they threw with heated zeal; they sped—
More, and more—to reach the ocean main.

Thus the boat of oranges, the slow,
Bearing all the welcome load would go
To the ship, to which in turn would throw
Other boatmen fish, and others bread,
While the ship within her womb would stow
Coals in hold still open, as if dead.

(122) Reply

It would seem that every émigré,
Hounded in the past, will now attempt
Proudly to prepare the way
To deliverance, no more dirempt
Of necessities. The men exempt
From the laws will cause no more delay.

Oranges, most notably delicious,
Are the emblems of a golden land,
Miracle of El Dorado, and—
Jesus' miracle of loaves and fishes ...
Will the exiled men achieve their wishes?
Resurrections ... who can say?

(123) Landscape

As at last, in single moment-blink,
Heaped from slopes and homes and pieces, ridges
Of the ancient heavens, broken bridges,
And from up above, by fate we think,
Struck by sunset, with its hues infused,
Riven up, and open, and accused—
Might a tragic hamlet-death ensue,

If into the wound there didn't go
From the sequent hour in scatter-flow
Falling drops of cooling blue
That are mixed with evening by the night,
So the heat that, fanned, had reached a height,
Soft, goes out, redeemed, set right.

Door and arch are tranquil as the day,
Clouds, transparent, came to sway
Over rows of houses pale
That had swallowed all the dark away;
Ah, but—sudden—from a moon a shine
Lightly glided through, as if, divine,
Archangelic sword had loosed a ray.

(123) Reply

We who live in little towns upstate,
Rural-life New Yorkers, Vestalites,
Know them well, the allegoric sites
Hinting of a pilgrim and his fate.
Breistadt, Johnson, Gifford, Church, and Cole,
McEntee, Durand, Kensett, and Heade:
These the Hudson River School had led,

Teaching of the pilgrim in the soul,
Tracing all the stages he will pass
Till what's doomed to wither as the grass
Be redeemed, nor drown in Swamp Despond,
See at eve a light-shaft, a Beyond,
Past the drum-and-trumpet storms that roll.

Tragedy, redemption, angel-sword
Are the tokens that proclaim the Lord,
Painting an apocalypse for all
Whom an act of God may well appall
Or, with sudden psalm of summer, bliss
Tender in a gesture not amiss.
If the sacred leave me scared and scarred,
Will to rise might stay benignly starred.

(124) Roman Countryside

From the cluttered town ('twould rather sleep,
Dreaming, peaceful, of the high hot spring)
Straight the Way of Graves the path will keep
To the Fever. Afterglance they fling,

Final farmhouse windows, angry-eyed.
Ever by the neck he has them, tied;
When he leaves—right, left, destruction wide—
Till he conjures up more breath, outside,

All his void to heaven-height to raise,
Looks around to see if he'll be met
By a window, beckons to the broad

Aqueducts to come, with friendly nod.
For his own, a heaven-gift he'll get:
Emptiness, ev'n longer than his days.

(124) Reply

Rilke-Malte, double Spendthrift Son,
Made a bold request when he would ask
That he not be loved: the poet-task
Meant dispensing with a benison.

Wandering unloved, alive, alone,
Would uncompromising light imply:
All would widen the unguided eye,
Waited-for behavior hateful grown.

Azrael, who's Death, the myriad-wing'd,
Filled with emptiness, the man would face.
Past the dragon, tail with world-life ring'd,

He, soul-opened, the Maqóm, the Place,
Would inhabit: that would mean to move.
Fire-refined, he'd seek and mettle prove.

(125) Song of the Sea

Primal waft of sea,
Sea wind by night,

You do not come to me;

By wakeful light,
One is aware that he
Will weather you:

Primal waft of sea
That breathes through
Only for olden stone
Space alone
Rends from afar in me ...

It feels you moan,

A striving tree
In moonlit blue.

(125) Reply

Sparrow on key,
Light finger whim,

Alert will be

To what in him
Is fluttering:
The cold of morn,

The day that in
The soul will break
When bird reborn
The herald charge
Will take,

The heart enlarge,

The gift begin,
The flood to sing.

(126) Night Travel

Saint Petersburg

Then with trotters moving speedily
(Black they were, the famous Orloff breed)
While behind high candelabra glee
Lay the townhouse fronts, renewed indeed,
Mute, not fit for any time of day,
We were traveling—no, passed, or flew—
'Round the palace-burden turning, too,
Toward the brisking wind of Neva Quai,

Forward forced across the wakeful night
That no earth or heaven can possess,
While unguarded gardens, urgent, might
Rise in Lyetni Sad's fermenting stress,
And the statue figures formed of stone,
Dwindling, contour weakened, each alone,
Vanished while we passed (our speed had grown)—

That's when suddenly the town
Ceased to be, at once admitting, too,
It had never been, but would pursue
Rest—a madman who the wild delusion
Simply dropped that led him to confusion—
And who felt a thought that many years
Plagued him with accumulating fears—
(No more thinkable!)—like granite-rock
From the empty, swaying, brain-case down
Fall, quite gone from vision and from talk.

(126) Reply

Suddenly the buildings disappear—
Merely artificial imposition!
This had truly been the hope-and-fear
Souls had felt. The mighty Peter's mission
Led him putatively to the harsh
War with Sweden: capturing an area
Filled with likely prospect of malaria,
He would build a city on that marsh.

Bronze, the horseman Peter in a storm,
Nightmare of a civil service clerk,
Bodied forth his perils in a form
That would quickly do an impish work,
Driving poor Yevgéni quite insane.
Death and danger ever seemed to lurk,
Seeping into harried-weary plasma
From the all-pervading gray miasma
Spread from ancient time upon the plain.

So the poet Pushkin grimly wrote,
Summing up his own and others' dream.
Gogol's poor Akaki of a coat
Fantasized, but with the hopeful gleam
After years of penny-pinching turned
To supposed reality, he learned
"Be" in Petersburg was merely "seem."
Stolen overcoat! Unholy thief:
Spectral ghost that, hidden in the mist,
Stealthy first, then with a fatal fist,
Gave the martyred heart a final grief!

(127) Parrot Park

Botanical Garden, Paris

Under the lindens from Turkey, at lawn-borders
    blooming,
Gentle-toned, homesick, and swaying, and shaken in
    glooming,
Breathe the macaws in their knowledge of lands, and
    they falter,
Though when they're gazing away there is naught
    they can alter.

Strange 'mid the busily-greening, as if they're
    parading,
They are adorning themselves, and self-pity
    unlading,
While, with their high-valued beaks made of jasper
    and jade,
Chewing gray food, they, rejecting bad taste, are
    dismayed.

Dull-colored doves will pick out what they'd rather
    cast off;
Scornful, the birds up above that incline from on
    high,
Squandering one, then the other near-emptying
    trough;

Rocking again, and then napping, then, widened of
    eye,
Playing, their tongues being darkened and eager to
    lie,
Scattered on footholds of chains. Are some viewers
    nearby?

(127) Reply: Stefan George's "My White Macaws"

My macaws of white have saffron yellow crowns and
    they
In the lattice-caging stay
Beckoning in slender rings
Not a call and not a song—
Slumber long—
Never do they spread their wings—
White macaws—each meditates—
Dreams of distant tree with dates.

(128) Parks

I

Unrestrainable the parks upthrong
From the scatter-vanish, soft and numb;
Overheaped with heavens, overstrong,
Given over, thus they overcome,

That on clear and level lawns they may
Spread themselves about and, too, withdraw,
Sovran in luxuriant display,
Sheltered, guarded so, by hidden law,

Royal grandeur, growing, more and more,
Inexhaustibly they will redeem,
Self-transcending, riches inward pour,
Purple, preening, pompous, and pristine.

(128) Reply

To genii or spirits of the hills
And souls of lonely places will the man
(If he be Wordsworth) call, and later can
Recall it and revive. The impulse fills

A tunesmith to peranimate the seen,
Perfuse it with the crimson beat he feels.
Laud animism: law of the ideals
Alembicated by a kenner keen.

A park becomes a person—or a town,
As Dublin came to be for witty Joyce,
The once and future perfect city choice,

Or Petersburg for Biély. 'Twould explode,
Yet poems, to this live-dead body owed,
In novel form were living laurel crown.

(129) Parks

II

Lightly by tree-lined lanes
Seized, to the left and right,
Following hints one gains
For lines of sight,

Suddenly you will go
To what's together-grown—
A water basin, low,
Four benches, stone—

Into a separate-set
Time that has left the land.
On pedestals made wet
Where nothing more will stand,

Deeply a sigh you heave,
Awaiting now,
While silver drippings that leave
The boat-dark bow

Already deem they own
You, and repeat the thought.
And you feel you are under stone
That hears, and you're moving not.

(129) Reply

The poet animist
With his wakening breath
Has been by Hypnos kissed,
Brother of Death.

The Lucy Wordsworth found
Had perturbing grace:
Streams' murmur-sound
Was in her face.

Beggars with Nature blent
Devoid of will
Were voicing an element
Muffled, still.

The contraries, living and dead,
Not well defined,
Have their border shed
In the forming mind.

On a ridge we tread
And are dizzied there,
As the living and dead
Blend in the air.

(130) Parks

III

The pond in able frame, the fishing pool,
To keep a secret one may well prefer
From kings. They stay enveiled, and as a rule,
At any moment maybe Monseigneur

Will walk across, and then a pond may want
To milden the monarchal whim or gloom
And from the marble borders newly vaunt
The carpets which the mirror-forms illume

When those are overdraped as in a square:
On ground of green—pink, silver, gray are there;
Kind-granted white, and blue light-touched with life,
And, too, the monarch and his charming wife,
While flowers in the edging taste the air.

(130) Reply

From life we turned to death, and next to art;
More problem-pairs appear: and here we start.
Does poetry unclothe a sleeping maid
Or cover her with woven-gold brocade?

When Shelley wrote, defending poesy,
He said that both are true. How can it be?
For answer, ponder long the Rilke pool,
Where transformation-faithfulness can rule.

Though mirrored colors brighter have become,
The painter is but Nature, air and sun.
If shapes are altered and made smoother, too,
'Tis Nature's framer, water, that we view.

The tender taste of Nature that we see
Is what the Mind attains in reverie.

(131) Parks

IV

Nature, noble and inducing awe,
As if hurt by random indecision,
Borrowed from these kings a greening law,
Blest herself, of table-baize a vision,

Heaping up her dream of trees, a bulge,
Swell, exaggerating verdant hues,
And the eves when lovers we indulge
Telling of them in the avenues—

All of this to paint with gentle brush
That to hold a smile, as lacquer bright,
Newly loosened from a hold might seem:

Nature's—lovely—showing not her might,
But a smile selected here to gleam
Thus upon a love-isle, rose-filled, lush,
Making it of yet a greater dream.

(131) Reply

One with eye remaking what is lent,
Reading through the text to what might be
Motivation, based on empathy,
So revivifies the element

That he'll thankful be for the reply
When a visitation, as by chance,
Lights the eye, incites the heart to dance:
Quiet, he will let it fill the eye.

When a sparrow lights upon a rail,
Iron, of an out-of-doors café,
I am his, so long as he will stay.

When a rabbit, stationed on my lawn,
Waits, to hear the songs before the dawn,
I am he, until the sky turn pale.

(132) Parks

V

Goddesses of galleries, allées,
Never quite believed-in deities,
Who are aging on their straight-cut ways,
Smiled upon at best, Diana-fays,
When the royals, in their veneries,

Like the wind that morning overraced,
Rising, hasting, making others haste—
Smiled upon at best but, if you please,

Gods not prayed to. Pseudonyms, we can
Rightly name them, under which a man
Hid himself, or bloomed, indeed might burn;
They would lightly nod and smiling turn,
Gods who merely, now and then, with ease

Grant what once they granted, for our pardon,
When the blooms in the delighted garden
Take away their stiff demeanor, cold:
When, from early shade, they trembling shake,
Promise after promise will they make,
Indistinct and limitless and bold.

(132) Reply: Alexander Pushkin's "Earliest Memories ..."

Earliest memories return to me:
So many carefree children in that school—
We were a rough, unruly family.

One teacher, using mildness for a tool,
Though looking humble in a homely dress,
Majestically would affirm her rule.

Surrounded by a crowd of us, no less
Would she continue speaking calmly, sweetly,
Chatting in a serene imperviousness.

I yet can see her headshawl, worn so neatly—
That, and those clear blue eyes, a brightened sky—
But from her talk I'd turn away discreetly.

I found that I was irritated by
Her brow austere, her tranquil lips and glance,
And, most of all, her holy talk, so high.

I shunned the calmness of her countenance;
I'd stubbornly distort her every saying,
Twisting away its clear significance.

And often, stealthily, would I be straying
Into the nearby garden's glorious gloom,
Under its arch of porphyry delaying.

The coolness of the shadows gave me room
To roam within my dream, so comforting,
So pure the pleasure: thoughts began to bloom.

I loved fresh waters, leafy whispering,
The blinding idols in the greening shade,
Immobile thought each face enlivening.

All that the sculptor had in marble made—
Sword, lyre, scroll, compass in their hands of white;
Wreath on a head; on shoulder, mantle laid—

These things all made a sweet, uncertain fright
Invade my heart, and tears of inspiration
The eyes would fill, so moving was their might.

Two statues of miraculous creation,
Of magic beauty, over me would tower:
Two demons, looking down from lofty station.

The first (the Delphic idol), in the flower
Of youth, was angry, filled with awful pride,
And seemed to seethe with otherworldly power.

The other was a female deified,
Sensual, doubtful, and duplicitous,
Enchanting demon, not to be denied.

Before them I would stand oblivious:
My heart—so young!—kept pounding, and a chill
Passed over me, my hair stood up, I was

Tormented, hungered darkly for the thrill
Of joys unknown. Despair and apathy
Enchained me, useless in my youth, until

I took to living lonely, quietly,
Bitterly brooding on the garden idols
Their spirit-shadow casting over me.

(133) Parks

VI

You feel, not one of all
The paths will stop and stay;
From abandoned steps will fall
Through a naught of inclination
Softly allured away,
All terraces to pass,
Paths crossing rocky mass;
Led, and slowed, they bend
To come where ponds are wide
Where them (to like allied)
The wealthy park will send

Through wealthy space: the one
That, with shine and re-shine sun,
Can pierce its ownmost things,
From which it on every side
Brings to itself what's wide
And, fleeing ponds that enclose,
For eve-fest cloud that glows,
Itself to heaven flings.

(133) Reply

Wind, in *Song of Sea*,
The dazed beholder found,
Open tore a space
Unknown within, as he
Listening watched the place
And savored alien sound.
So here the road-surround
Draws into it a *where*
That's wider than the air,
And deeper than her moans,
Yet which the pathway owns
Because of where it's been
And what it yet can be.

A space within I bear
That can a stranger greet
And open roughly tear
From things unwilled, unknowns,
A thing unbounded there,
And room will come to meet
What you may bring within
That opens me.

(134) Parks

VII

Naiad shapes in fountain basins are
Mirrored where, instead of bathing, they
As if drunken float, distorted, rocked;
The allées, through balustrades, afar,
Would appear forbidden, locked.

Leaves fall ever wetter and more pale
Through the air, and on the steps abide,
Every birdcall seemingly decried,
And envenomed every nightingale.

Even spring itself can give no more,
Shunned by faithless bushes that deride;
Glum, reluctant fragrances outpour
Jasmines that survive but stand aside,

Old, and with decrepitude immixed—
Midges moving with you while you go,
As if, when you change direction so,
All would be effaced, erased, and nixed.

(134) Reply

Number seven in the suite, the song
Called to mind a printed picture with
Seven Ages of a Man. The pith:
Up, then down; and nothing lasting long.

Crawling, then erect, now deathward bent,
Thus we alter, by the bell-shaped curve
Ordered to obey, that shape to serve:
Oedipal, the riddle-wisdom lent.

Shall we think of it as tragedy?
I recall the Gothic-lettered chart
Hanging in the hall. My father's heart

Seemed but little saddened. Wasn't he
Merely realistic? Rise and fall:
Nothing's part of anything at all.

(135) Portrait

So that from the grand, renouncing face
None of her afflictions great would fall,
Through the tragedy she's bearing, tall,
Lovely withered trait-bouquet with grace;
Features wildly bound: near-loosened, those;
She at times, will drop—her tuberose—
Just a little smile behind to leave.

So, abandoned, she will walk away,
Weary, with the lovely hands, but blind,
Knowing there are things they cannot find,—

And imagined things are what she'll say:
Whimsied, willful, where a fate will sway;
Meaning from her soul are they assigned,
Bursting out uncannily, upthrown,
Like the outcries of a stone—

And, her chin raised high, she will allow
All these words at once again to fall;
Nothing stays; there's not a one of all
Fit for pained reality that begs;
For her ownmost property,
She, a leaning vessel reft of legs,
Must contain, above what people see
And the parting hour of eve.

(135) Reply

She would bear a lorn and tragic face,
Bravely try a smile that's yet estranged,
With her frangible and bitter grace
Threatened by disorder, disarranged.

Awkwardness of gesture may reveal
Mask and stature merely are assumed.
She is playing, making up the day.
In a world of would-be will, the real
Is by brief uncanny acts illumed,
As a darkened room by moonlight ray.
Mental wobbler, swaying, she will stride,
Chin raised high in pride.

Part of her is tragic, yet I see
Bits of quite pathetic comedy.
Costume parties make us laugh and, too,
Humor comes when we are "seeing through"
Guises no one's meant to penetrate.
Ev'n though high society may rue
Having to admit that it's a ruse
We the great pretender will refuse
Deep respect accruing to the great.

Force mechanical encroaching on
Living flexibility is wit.
I don't simply make a joke of it;
Farce, however, cannot quite be gone
From a guise-machine, expression wan.

(136) Morning in Venice

dedicated to Richard Beer-Hofmann

Princely pampered windows ever see
What at times the city deigns to try,
Heaven's gleam to meet repeatedly
By the feeling of a flooding high:

So, self-molding, nowhere will it be.
Every morning opals early shows
That she yesterday had borne; in rows
Mirrored forms from the canal break free,
Bring the last time back to memory,
Finally surrendering, fall down

Like a nymph whom Jove is welcoming,
Tinkling pretty pendant on her ear:
That's San Giorgio Maggiore here—
Smiling Venice wears the charming thing.

(136) Reply

"For she doth hang upon the cheek of night
Like a rich jewel in an Ethiop's ear."
So charmingly the Bard of Avon might
Depict the way his Juliet would appear

Enframed by Romeo who'd glad become
An Ethiop, that the maid might hang on him.
Alas, the tone of smitten seraphim,
For all the jewel must convey of bright,
Will only make the hue of coming night
Yet deeper seem of lovers' halidom.

(137) Late Fall in Venice

The city plays no more the role of bait
That every day emerging wills to catch.
The tones of palaces of glass don't wait
A gazer. Summer hangs beyond the latch

Of garden gate: a heap of marionettes
Head foremost, wearied, made away with, slain.
But depth, 'mid sylvan skeletons, begets
A rising will, as if above night's pain

The General of Ocean Sea would double
The galleys in the arsenal, alert,
The coming morning breeze with tar to trouble

By nearing fleet where sailors strike the oar,
And suddenly, all standards flying pert,
Sails with the wind, in radiance and at war.

(137) Reply

A city of disguise and masquerade
Is tired of dancing, wearied by the dawn,
For much too long, in autumn, having played
The courtesan, new costumes putting on

And doffing in a wild, unending change.
The hues are waning, and her smile is wan.
So nature makes her way, to disarrange
Reminders of the carnival long gone.

We feel a will awaken 'mid the trees,
A force unfathomed, boreal abode:
I see the Alder King, from colder north,

Avenging, warlike, madly sally forth.
But winter's brightened by the brilliancies
Of southern sun, that welcome light yet sowed.

(138) San Marco

Venice

Within this inwardness, that as if hollowed
Is vaulted, turning round in golden smalt,
Round-cornered, smooth, whose value we exalt,
The darkness of the State is halted, swallowed,

And secretly upraised, a balancing
With light, that in whatever things draw near
So multiplies, they nearly disappear—.
You even wonder: are they vanishing?

Harsh gallery you'd like to push away,
That as a cavern passage near the light
Of vaulting hangs: you recognize the ray

Of healing outlook: somehow, though, your sight
Measures the weary while, with little love,
By the four horses high that stand above.

(138) Reply

Pervading fancy-light that counteracts,
Though not entirely, mighty, darker forces
Embodied in Constantinople horses
Of iron, stol'n in war, discordant facts:

I, in San Marco, felt that tension, too.
A perfect group of skillful melodists
Were playing while the sunlight dimmed the mists;
I at a table wrote, enjoyed the view,

The tunes, the skipping pigeons everywhere,
The sweetness of the partly salty air.
The hours had passed ... The manager came out,

Polite—his helper, though, with sulky pout,
Plus bulging muscles. Would I pay a fee
For table rent? Indeed!—*so* willingly!

(139) A Doge

Foreign envoys viewed them in their greed,
Saw them aiding him in every act,
Rousing him to grandness, but indeed
Placing round the dogedom, in their tact,

Spies, confiners, guards, increasingly,
Lest he crush them, and themselves be blamed
Feeding him (so men have lions tamed);
Thus their caution. Yes, but he,

Aided by a semi-uttered thought,
Wasn't wise to this and didn't seek
Greater power. What the Signory

Thought it forced and cleverly had wrought
He had done. In that gray head (not weak)
All was won. His face would let you see.

(139) Reply

Everything is won, yet all is lost:
Lion-mouthed, each mailbox that I saw,
Where the free-for-all, the Spying Law
Let informer-messages be tossed.

When the Party turns you to a spy
Watching other Party members, all,
Such betrayal will the state befall
As will mean men's dignity must die.

Lion-mawed, the law of fear devours
Every pretense that our moral pow'rs
Can withstand the traitor, thieving sneak.

Love is strong, deceiving fear is weak.
Who declare suspicion's iron rule
Are themselves befooled by whom they fool.

(140) The Lute

I am the lute. Would you my body-state
Portray, its curved and carven outline pure,
Say it is like a fully ripe, mature
Fig, and you may exaggerate

The dark that you can see within. I take
From Tullia my darkness. Yet her shame
Was not so great. Her brightened hair would make
Light, as a bright-lit room. And she would claim

Back, from my surface, tone she would prefer
Into her face, and she would sing to me.
I to her frailty gave a melody:
My inwardness was, in the end, in her.

(140) Reply

The art she made will take the shame away
From darkness in the heart, the light of hair
Shine with a vibrancy of strings in air;
The body, not opaque, will play

Soundings whereof the soul in living wood
Had unawake yet dreamed to make aware
The sylvan limbs that quivered in the air
Abashed of aspen when the tree had stood.

Black sun, the cavity will amplify
The lonely overtones that underlie
Whatever muted in the mind had stayed,
Now come alive in light of lute I played.

(141) The Adventurer

I

When, among the sundry ones who *were,*
He, the Sudden, came, who but *appeared,*
Gleams that thoughts of peril would bestir
Shone about him, in the space well-cleared,

Which he smiling walked across, that he
Might pick up, polite, the duchess' fan,
Warmest thing! that he, that eager man,
Wanted to see fall. When nobody

To the window-niche would go with him
(Where the parks in dreamy world and dim,
When he'd point them out, would seem to rise)
He at card games, in the interim,
Played and won—while people's eyes

On the man their focus keen would keep,
Whether skeptical, or tenderly;
These you'd also in the mirror see.
He had planned, today as well, no sleep

(Too much like the last long night) and spare
Looks of which a reckless man disposes,
As if he'd engendered, with the roses,
Children being nurtured who knows where.

II

In the days (but no such days were known)
When the flood to keep its deepest loss
Fought with him, as if 'twere not his own,
Pushing him to reach the height of stone,
To the highest vaulting tried to toss,

Suddenly, of many one: a name
Struck him that he long ago had borne.
And he knew once more: the lives, they came
When he lured them: they would soar,

Come in flight; still warm, the dead ones' lives
(Mind impatient, threatened while he strives)
He, in midst of them, lived yet;
Or not-lived-out lives, unfinished gift—
These he knew and proved that he could lift:
New, the meaning they would get.

It would seem no place could safely bear him,
And he trembled: I'm—I seem—
Then, next moment you might well compare him
To the darling of a queen.

Always there was Being to be had:
These, the fates of many a captured lad,
Which, as if too menacing to dare,
Folk would abrogate, forswear,

He took up, tore loose; within, they teem;
For he knew he'd be obliged the grave
Of the ones surrendered to disseize;
Fragrance of their possibilities
Lay again in open air and brave.

(141) Reply: Nikolay Gumilev's "Cross"

When card after card told me lie after lie
I felt no success in attempts to get drunk.
Cold stars, 'mid the terror of March in the sky,
Paled one, then another, and fainting had sunk.

In coldness, in madness, my starving heart sank.
I knew that the game was no more than a dream:
"This card—let it cover the whole bloody bank!"
The card proved a loser. That settled my scheme.

I needed fresh air. Snowy dawn. Ah, so tender
The wandering shade on the softness that now—
Gold cross to my lips I would hold—in surrender—
I fell to my knees then, I hardly know how.

"I want to breathe freely, like stars to live purely:
Your rod, Lady Poverty, sister of loss,
I'll take! I will wander, beg bread! I will surely
Bring healing, redeem—by the aid of the cross."

A pause ... and at once, 'mid the loud jubilation
All stopped. They were silently rising, bestirred:
I entered the hall in a flaming elation
And onto the card put my cross. Not a word.

(142) Falconry

Being emperor, by secret deed
You will oversee and show your might;
So the chancellor the tow'r at night
Entered, saw the treatise he must heed:
Princely play of quill, a splendid sight

Which devoted scribes, bent down, prepared;
He himself had, in a hall withdrawn,
Many times and nights until the dawn
For the unaccustomed creature cared,

New and strange and in a férment wild.
Plans that, growing, rose and heart beguiled
He'd avoid and call frivolities,
Even from his tender memories
Purest inner empathies
Turning, for the fawned-upon

Falcon's sake, whose heated blood and fret
He was not permitted to forget.
So he felt himself as if upraised,
When the bird, whom all the lords had praised,
From the hand outflung arose emblazed,
Spring together-felt in morning, fierce,
Angel-like, his heron-prey to pierce.

(142) Reply

Myriad falcons: one with wings, and one
Called the chancellor, and then the scribes.
Many ruled endure the ruler-fun.
Are the hawking calls but mocking gibes?
Heavy labor: is it ever done?

First the worker must on treadmill run ...
Then the chancellor is feeling freed
By the diver's high-endearing deed—
Moment brief—and ended when begun!
Art and sport at call of sovran pow'r
Let the trained attain their golden hour.
Sheremiétiev sent a serf to learn
Grand Italian singing; she'd return,
One among three hundred thousand slaves,
Take applause, and bow to cheers and waves ...
Queen or puppet? Double is the dow'r.

Talent scouts in China went to scour
'Round the countryside and bring the best
Two or three who passed the rigid test
To the capital: in the ballet
These would work their youthful lives away
For the People and triumphant tow'r
At the mighty sovereign's behest.

(143) **Program of Bullfights**

in memoriam Montez, 1830

Since he, nearly little, broke away
From the fights that ear and eye abhor
And the will of headstrong picador
And the ribbon-hookpole as in play

Took as well, they'd mightily assist,
Making native storminess more great,
Heaping up from ancient sable hate,
Baleful head compressed into a fist,

Aimed at not just anyone at all,
No, the bloody neck-hook hoisted high,
Back behind the lowered horns, and why?
Well he'd known eternally: to fall

On the one in rose-mauve silk and gold
Who had quickly turned and, like a bee-
Swarm, as if he too were pained to see,
Letting through, below the arms he'd hold

High, the conquered bull. His glances hot
Yet again will, lightly guided, rise,
And as if, outside, the circle sought
Shield against the light and dark of eyes
And of every eyelid-strike that vies,

Ere he can, indifferent, free of spite,
Indolently, and as if 'twere light,
On the great, capacious, wide-unrolled
Wave that rose, before the stroke unfold,
Nearly gently, dagger strike aright.

(143) Reply

Convoluted syntax here we see;
Often we will savor it some more.
It is high in Rilke's favor for
Incremental tension. We will store
Complicated thought, then suddenly

Comprehend the secret, as, e.g.,
Long-accumulated jealousy
That, if envied object it should strike,
Less importance will acquire, belike,
Than the fascination of the growth
Of a ramifying upas tree.

How the thing will tend we need to know,
See how well the venomed tree will grow.
There's another trademark strategy
Aiding in our planned perplexity:

He, him, his, the one, at times befool.
Have they antecedents? That is vague.
Grammar teachers view it as a plague:
Rulers—with a straightedge they would rule.

But when victor, victim blended are,
When the dreamer and the dream are one,
Man with plan entwined in ricercar,
We must be with clear distinction done.

(144) Don Juan's Childhood

Almost decisively, his slimness made
A thing no lady broke, an archer-bow;
At times, the brain no longer to evade,
A longing through the face would, sudden, show—

Attraction to a woman passing by,
In whom, for him, an old, strange form would grow:
He smiled. He was no longer one who'd cry,
Brood darkly, or forget himself, let go.

While new self-confidence he'd not neglect,
A comfort, if a nearly twisted one,
To bear their full-eyed gaze he had begun,
That him would stir, and deeply would affect.

(144) Reply: Nikolay Gumilev's "Don Juan"

I simply, haughtily, will dream of this:
To grab the oar, to mount the horse, to while
Away the time, my boredom to beguile,
Unnumbered waiting maiden mouths to kiss,

With vows devout in later age a Chris-
tian to become, monastic-meek, and pile
The ashes on my head!—in humble style
To feel the cross, that heavy burden-bliss!

And yet, 'mid orgies once, more dead than quick,
Sane suddenly, and pale, a lunatic
In rare remission of a mental smother,

I might remember: useless, barely human,
I never had a child with any woman
And, as for men, there's none I call my brother.

(145) Don Juan's Choice

And the angel neared: You must attend;
Make yourself prepared, as I require.
I command that every man transcend
Deeds that to the best and sweetest friend
Bitterness occasion, damage dire.
True, a little better you might love
(Interrupt me not; you err indeed),
Yet you're ardent, and 'tis writ above:
You will many ladies lead
To the loneliness that deep
Entryway for these will keep.
Those I show to you, admit:
They, than Héloïse more fit,
Her, outshouting, will exceed.

(145) Reply

A seeker learns from alien worlds with ease
To find delightful costume-role to don.
Those who may yet excel an Héloïse
Will get the best of training from Don Juan.
In Grecian hell would Mephistopheles
One eye, one tooth, the Graeae-guise put on.
And Helen classical amenities
Will teach to Faust before her ardor's gone.
Alchemical Homunculus with ease
Will sing for Galatea hymn of swan;
Odysseus, the master of the seas,
Calypso-lips command in love at dawn.
A wise advising angel, if you please,
Desire may introduce on Eden-lawn.

(146) Saint George

She had called to him throughout the night
And in supplication kneeled, the weak,
Wakeful maid. What does that dragon seek?
He watches, why? I'm baffled in my fright.

And when he'd broken forth from morning gray
On fallow land, bright-helmed with hauberk-ray,
He saw her, in a spell of sad amaze,
Upon her knees, beseeching upward gaze

Bent to the brilliance that was he.
Radiant, then, away along the lands
He sprang, huge weapon held in both his hands,
Into peril, openly,

Far too frightful, yet he'd begged for this.
And she kneeled more kneelingly, her hands
Firmly clasped—we'd hope he understands—
Yet the point of all of it she'd miss:

He must go beyond, the man her fair,
Ready heart from godly, guiding light
Downward rends. Apart from battle bright
Stands, as towers stand away, her prayer.

(146) Reply

Lady stepped aside; it had to be.
Fighting serpent-dragons of the sea,
George, and Typhon-fighter, deified,
Gazed on Chaos, lordly, steely-eyed.

When Marduk split Tiamat apart,
He the pattern stamped, to win the heart
Of the monarchs of the Middle East
Ancient state, where combat rarely ceased.

Kill the snake and build the Babel Tow'r:
Mother-deep defeated, for your dow'r
You shall have a maiden who will kneel,
Tribute to your fatal blade reveal.

We forget: a Bible concubine
Served as slave, her chosen life-design
Set aside, with 'kneeling' the decree
Meaning she'd not act but merely be

Mother of a warrior who'd turn
Rod to serpent, show how rulers earn
Staff and orb and scepter, tribute take
From the long since conquered water-snake.

(147) Lady on a Balcony

Wind-wrapt, out she'd come, and impulse-willed,
As if drawn, a light into the light;
While the room appears now polished bright,
Open doors behind are filled

Darkly, background of a cameo,
Through the edges letting glimmers go;
You would think there'd been no evening till
She had come, upon the railing, still,

Just a little something to lay by,
Just the hands, to be a light entire:
So the sky from row of houses higher
Reaches, needs to move away, be high.

(147) Reply

In a gesture, we may tell a geste,
Lore of high adventure dreamed, where we
Image ample virtuality:
Carriage, bearing, and deportment best.

To a lazy turning we advert:
In the curving of a hand Rodin
The corporeality of man
Read into mentality alert.

Like a rounded phrase, a body part
Captivates the heart in hymn, and may
Render in the field a roundelay
Lit by altar of a lover's art.

(148) Encounter on the Chestnut Allée

To him had been the entryway's dark green
More cool than silken robe around that he
Might take, arrange; and there might also be
Far, at the other end, transparent, seen,

Out of the greening sun and greening panes,
A single figure all in white
And lighted up, that it quite far might stay
And finally, when lights were bent away,
With every step would fade from sight,

Bright alteration bearing, so to say,
That shy, in blond, behind had run.
But shades would suddenly more deep become,
And eyes, brought near, lay open as the day

Illumining a new, distincter face
That stayed, as in a portrait bound
At just the moment when she left that place:
First was it always, then no longer found.

(148) Reply

She has appeared to me a nymph in leaves,
Made of their flicker in the morning dark
That of the tree-lined way within the park
Painted a scene in which one half-believes,

A flicker-figure that the mist enwreathes
Much more than does the barely waking sun;
Had ancient making of a myth begun
At such a time? when earth but half-outbreathes
The mercy-dew, the cool not done,

Uneager to undo the misty, dim
Somnambulance of passion moving him
Who, having dreamed at ease, would travel far
To glimpse, with youthful and with impish whim,
Schooled by a tutelary Lar,

What could emerge and, vanishing, would be
A dream that memory might sheathe
And keep, a sylph that if the sun-heat seethe
Will rise—the eyes! the sign that she
Is no more portraiture than he.

(149) The Sisters

Same, the possibilities that they
Differently bear and activate,
Different times embody through the way
In the chambers twinned they walk or wait.

One would hope the other one to aid,
Giving her a little rest when tired;
Bonds between relations, though, are made
Harder by a nearness undesired

When, as earlier, respectively,
They, on the allée, don't hesitate
One to guide and one be guided, see?
Ah, they differ in their pace and gait.

(149) Reply

with a bow to Frank Sulloway

Siblings differ more than you'd suppose
Even if inheriting the "same."
Ordering of birth will soon disclose
Each is planning with a different aim.

Firstborn child is cherished and will be
Lured to follow in parental ways.
Younger ones, competing, likely see
Other means to win the people's praise.

Middle children try to mediate
(Think of Gandhi, Martin Luther King),
Older, younger doubly counterweight:
So they find a role that praise may bring.

Families are many-movement games,
Recognition and approval sought
By contrasting strategies and claims
Molding what inheritance had brought.

(150) Piano Practice

The summer hums. The noon will make you tired.
Bewildered, she the freshness of her dress
Inhaled, then laying down, as they required,
Impatience for the real, that, as she'd guess,

Tomorrow, or tonight, could yet befall—
Was maybe even here, though hidden still;
Before the windows, high and having all,
The pampered park the girl at once could fill

With feeling: and she stopped, glanced out, put down
Her hands, and hoped she'd find a good long book.
That fragrant jasmine plant!—she wouldn't look;
It made her sick; she pushed it with a frown.

(150) Reply

The études and the exercises and
Even the pieces loved and savored well
Self-confidence can weaken more than hand
Or heart: it seems unlearned, the magic spell

That suddenly might put them in our grasp ...
And why? The teacher always will assign
What's meant for minds more finely skilled than
    mine
Is now—so I'll *advance*. But ah! to clasp

A mastered work as a reward I earned!
That fresh delight of life need not be spurned:
Assign me, pray, what I may avidly
Perform—make master-dream reality.

(151) Girl in Love

That window's why, I'd say,
My waking's been so light.
I thought I'd waft away.
How wide, my life today?
And where begins the night?

I'd almost thought the blue
Around was naught but I;
I look the crystal through,
Deep, darkened, muted sky.

Even the stars I could
Within embrace; my heart—
It feels so large: I would
Gladly from him now part

Whom I've perhaps to love,
Perhaps to hold begun.
Alien, the writing of
My fate, a something done.

So deep, I'm under this
Unendingness downlaid;
In fragrant meadow-bliss,
Forward and backward swayed,

I call, and fear as well
That one will seize the call
And in another's spell
I'll be, and I will fall.

(151) Reply

The reader's eye may start
To dampen even while
He hears the loving heart
And has begun to smile.
O poet's double art!

I've never been so wise,
When loving, as the girl.
Will doubleness defies
That sets the mind awhirl.
The fear I drave away
To wakened heart returned
To shake in shining day,
A jinn that inward burned.

The reason love is twinned
With sorrow-suffering
Is not that we have sinned,
But so we learn to sing,

With David, dirge and psalm:
The loved one, being all,
Appears, and we are calm;
Absconds, and we may fall.

To love is hard: to risk
A gash, with scar and more.
The Janus-basilisk
Will guard the starry door.

(152) Inwardness of Roses

Where for this "in" may be
An "out"? Upon what ache
Put linen tenderly?
What heavens mirrored, free,
Upon the inner lake
Of all these open roses,
Without a care, we see:
In looseness nothing closes
They lie so tranquilly
No trembling hand would rend them
Though they can scarce contain
Themselves; they're letting go
Overfull, overflow
Over the inner domain
During the days when they seem
Fully, more fully to close,
Till the summer a room of rose
Will become, and a room of dream.

(152) Reply

I see them, twins that lie
In a summer flowerbed.
They are sisters to the eye
That can tell how siblings vie
Though enclosed in drowsihead.
Sprung forth form a central root
In a time when the wild had sung
They will not be rendered mute
While the Tree of Eden's young.
One the Poet's, the other is mine.
They are languages: had you guessed?
In my ginkgo-leaved soul are they blest.
As the grass to the god will incline,
Prostrate, before the breeze,
To bend, to extend, and to rest,
So the speech-modes in equal ease
Of the evening their dreams entwine.

(153) Portrait of a Lady from the 'Eighties

Waiting stood she by the draperies
Taken up, dark satin hue,
Where we passionate luxuriancies
Clustering above may view

Since the time when older maiden years
Switched with newer, as when aging nears;
Under high-tiered hair, she tired appears,
To the crimping robes unused, one fears.
As if, curtain-hid, one overhears

She is homesick, plan unclear where age
Might her life's direction pull:
Likely not as on a novel's page,
Swept away, of fate-awareness full—

If one only might in casket lay
Something with the scent, to wearied mind,
Of a lulling and remembered day;
If one in a diary would find

A beginning, fresh, that wouldn't grieve
One with nonsense and with lies annoyed;
If one might a single petal leave,
Red, within a heavy pendant-void

Moved with every breath that she would take;
If a gesture from a window beckoned,
This thin hand, the new-beringed, she reckoned,
Surely months of comfort could awake.

(153) Reply

Sixteen-eighties, maybe? Do you think
I am jesting? Merely irony:
That's the only wit that I can see.
Into depth of solitude they sink

Who, as in *The House of Seven Gables*,
Lead a life as picture, statue, image,
While the role of agent, that enables,
These will flee, too frail for active scrimmage,
Fit for dressing rooms and breakfast tables.
Hephzibah, and Lady Nameless here,
As a part of properties are born.
Stranded on their lands, they will endear
Only insofar as they adorn.

Gone is now the silken, crimping gown;
Cruel mode will rule with crippling twists:
Tiptoe-heels, with risk of crashing down,
Earn the livings of chiropodists.

Plastic surgeries reshaping more
Than the knives of hapless Frankensteins,
Florida will have the magic lore
Lending timeless youth in laser lines.

Ah, but it is out of place to preach!
Rather, we are sought for sympathy.
Come, Pygmalion; kiss the maiden, reach
Heart with hand—too long the victim, she.

(154) Lady before a Mirror

Like a spice, with sleeping potion blent,
Gently she dissolves in limpid-flow
Mirror her demeanor, wearied so;
Smile entirely to the image lent.

She is waiting till the flowingness
Rises up and out; then loosened hair
In the mirror, she the wondrous bare
Shoulders raising from the evening dress,

Drinking from her picture, still. She drinks
What a lover would in tumult view,
Testing, full of doubt; she beckons, thinks

Now of the maid, when mirror-background shows
Lights, and the cabinets, and then she knows
Gloom of a latter hour, in pallid hue.

(154) Reply

The dark and light are fighting in her face.
The smile attempts the rigor to unfreeze,
But fixity of eye may kill her ease,
Mobility, the center of her grace.

The letter of expression would she seize,
But spirit has no dwelling in a place;
The former newborn life would fain erase;
The latter lives in whims' velleities.

Before the breath appeared on primal seas,
The dull of death exulting to replace
With tidings of the life within the breeze,

The depth as under rigid carapace
Had never felt that tenderest embrace.
Wind, water, sunlight: best of syzygies.

(155) The Gray-Haired Lady

Ladies, white, in the midst of today,
Listen and laugh, and they plan for tomorrow;
Off to the side, people, casual, weigh
Slowly their versions of care and of sorrow,

Dealing with how and the when and the why;
Sometimes you'll hear them begin, "In my view—"
Yet, in her cap of lace, kept spry,
She is a model of confidence who

Seems quite aware that they err, these and all.
Likewise her chin, when we see it fall,
Leans on white coral that fastens the shawl
Which 'round about her brow is bound.

Once, though, in midst of a laugh, she will shake
Out of her high-springing eyelids, awake,
Gaze that a difficult statement will make:
From a hidden drawer may a lady take
What pretty inherited gems are found.

(155) Reply

It's paradigmatic, this anecdote.
In his portraits and tales of the high sublime
Or in caricature we repeatedly note
The concluding surprise of the paradigm.

Sometimes ridiculous, always clever,
Deeply affecting more often than not,
Punchline's arriving, designed to dissever
Lethargic habit from startling thought.

People are speaking; they laugh and they dream,
And their whimsy, caprice, may appear to be
The predictable, silly, continued theme
That the lady refutes, who'll more deeply see.

Refutations are lacking; instead: a surprise.
No philosophy shines in the lady's eyes,
But the joy in a wealth that the sages despise
Will assoil—and assail what they say, the wise.
It is money makes you free.

(156) The Bed

Let them think dissolved in private woe
Will the thing that one had fought for be.
Theater is here: no farther go.
Curtain ripped away, you'll quickly see

Step, before the chorus of the nights
That began a vast, unending song,
Plain, their fateful hour of rising blights;
Garment they will rend, lamenting long,

For the sake of yet another hour,
Warded off, in background rolling now;
Alien, it had taken calming power
Quite away; but they to it must bow;

For it was the time when she, compelled,
In the one she loved at first had found
What was threatening and strongly bound
And, as in a beast, withdrawn, withheld.

(156) Reply

Greeks, we learn, would write their tragedies
In the form of sequences, to show,
In their chosen form of trilogies,
How our woes through generations grow.

Through the generations of our days,
Even more of sorrow-hoarded nights,
We repeatedly the question raise
Why recur the worst of sordid blights.

Repetition is itself the clue:
Vainly we replay the tale inscribed
In the wrinkles of the brain and view
Rabid habits that the mind imbibed.

Gravid yet, the tragedy in mask,
As in ancient Greece, today is played.
Veiled, the query that one fears to ask:
Half-concealed, the mummers are betrayed.

(157) The Stranger

Never caring what the neighbors thought—
Whom he, wearied, asked no more—again
Off he went, lost, leaving what he mought,
Hanging on the nights of travel then

Differently than any night of love.
Wondrously he'd held a vigil of
Heavens; covered up by strength of star,
They together bent the narrow-far,
Altering in warring push and shove;

Other nights when, moonlit and bestrewn,
Villages with kept, protected boon
Had surrendered; or, on sheltered ways,
Parks that noble pile and home had shown,
Where, a moment, had his favor grown,
Knowing deeplier one nowhere stays;
Then he'd see, near neighbor bend or bay,
How the bridge and path and landscape lay;
City, where exaggeration plays.

Wisely all of this he, undesiring,
Had abandoned, deed thought better done
Than to have possessions, fame, or fun.
But in foreign squares there had been one
Bowl of daily trodden fountain-stone
Which at times appeared to be his own.

(157) Reply

I would focus on the fountain bowl.
Here's a man uncaught by property,
Wandering the yondest, footloose, free,
Who would own it, enigmatic soul.

Resting, prior to his moving on,
Here he might have stopped to wash his feet
And could tell the people he would meet
Where he next would go, who'd soon be gone;
Stars in mind arise before the dawn.

(158) The Arrival

Was, in the wagon's way, this sudden swing?
And was it in the view when lookers could
Note in the field, near where the bluebells stood,
Baroque-style angels, memories to bring,

Perceived them, held them, and let go, before
The castle park around the journey closed
And brushed against and overhung it, posed—?
Then quickly opened. For it was the door,

The gate, that now, as calling them to go,
Urged them with lengthened front to make the turn
It stood behind. Upglancing went a glide

Of glass door sideward, and a greyhound stern
Would urge them upward, while its nearer side
It dragged down level steps to wait below.

(158) Reply

Unfixed transition-state he would convey;
Transitive, tending to an action, and
Transient and evanescent—what's at hand
Fled from the grasp that moments might waylay.

The moment of surprise—a theme that we've
Addressed before; a tension, sudden switch,
While we are puzzled, not yet seeing which
Direction will our expectation thieve.

To lack attachment!—that had been the goal
Of all the goalnessness our wander-soul
At once had aimed for, and yet presupposed.

A bafflement, a prospect undisclosed—
What we who live within a world presume
Our destiny by right: horizon-room.

(159) The Sundial

Seldom watchers of the moisture-rot
Reach beyond the garden shades—where heard
Are the raindrops each by other, bird
Wand'rer sings—to column brought
Where cilantro, marjoram have wrought
Fragrance, that the sun-hours may be shown;

Only when a lady (by a servant
Followed), in her broad-brimmed hat observant,
Bends to look, with shadow thrown,
Has the dial quiet grown—.

Or when rain of summer's coming by,
Rising in the waving movement high
Of the treetops, will it pause and slow;
For the time it cannot indicate
That will start, in fruit- and flower-state,
Suddenly in garden-house to glow.

(159) Reply

He is not a moralistic poet,
Yet a moral's waiting 'round the corner.
Of didactic poetry the scorner
Cannot mind although he'll know it—
Nor will ever feel we need a warner.
For the lesson he'll implicit make.

If you'd emulate the lively dial,
Best adopt a varied living style;
Be observant every hour
And diversify your power.

Shades of nature and of human act
Both may complicate the shadow-fact;
You will learn the time to rest and wake,
Motion that rewards or that eludes
Indication, and your changing moods
Cue from multiple conductors take.

(160) Drowsy Poppies

Apart, blooms in the garden evil sleep,
In which the ones who, urged there secretly,
Found love of younger mirrorings to be
Shown willing, open, and concave, and deep,

And dreams, that with the newly roused-up masks
Walked more gigantic, striding in cothurns—:
It all is held in these, uplifted flasks
Of yielding stems, that keep the seedling-urns

(After they side-inclining buds have borne
And meant to fade) shut fast, to nestle:
Their calyxes, befringed, asunder torn,
That feverishly gird the poppy-vessel.

(160) Reply

Hypnos, Thanatos bear Sárpedon
Wounded from the battlefield away.
Sleep and Death, the brothers twain are they;
Let us ponder well; we'll soon be gone:

Morpheus both love and hate will spawn.
Let the metamorphoses of day
Into night, that vanish with the dawn,
Blind us not, be warned, to morning ray.

Circe, all too siren-like, will say
Charming word, which heard, we're putting on
Shapes of peril, panoply of play
Fatal ev'n to satyr, pan, and faun.

(161) Flamingoes

Botanical Garden, Paris

As in a Fragonard they mirrored show
No more the white and carmine we commend,
As when a person might present a friend
And say, She woke from sleep just now. They go,

Arising, to the green, they're standing, pure,
On stalks of red, and lightly turn around,
Together blooming, as in flow'r bed found:
Than Phrynë more seductive, they allure,

Until of eyes the pallor may abide
In softness, where the fruit-red, black will hide
When, downward turned, the neck of each may glide.

Quick envy—shrieking through the aviary!
But they, amazed, have stretched, and now they
      stride
Alone into their own Imaginary.

(161) Reply

Flamingo-proud will Phrynë now appear
Before the Areopagus, the court.
Is it a stratagem of last resort
That she'll disrobe before the judges here?

And did it really happen? Scholars fear
Idomeneus of Lampsacus' tome
Cannot be trusted. Jean-Léon Gérôme,
However, made the painting wholly clear.

At any rate, what no one will dispute
Is that her beauty left the viewer mute:
She'd sculpted been as Aphrodite, and

A statue of herself, we understand,
Was later made by famed Praxiteles.
And yet she failed to tempt Xenocrates.

(162) Persian Sunflower

The lauding of the rose to you may seem
Too loud for your companion. Therefore take
The beautifully broidered plant. Now make
With urgent sunflow'r whisper louder theme

Than nightingale, who at her favored place
Can prize the rose with cries, yet knows her not.
Behold: sweet-worded sentences well-wrought
Stand thick together in unsevered grace;
From vowels' invigilated violet
Outbreathed, through quiet heaven-bed they've
        met—:

Before the quilted foliage will they close,
Clear-outlined stars toward silken vines of rose:
Immingled so, it well might swim away ...
Vanilla, cinnamon, the silent day.

(162) Reply

The daffodil, bright eye befringed,
The tulip, crimson-passioned, -singed,
Enclasping residue of black,
The rose, by breath of heaven tinged:

In Háfiz' lines we never lack
A splendid emblem of the wrack
Of lovers who with trouble cope,
The blissful kiss, the grand attack.

But medieval singers' hope
Had missed the foreign heliotrope:
America was not yet known;
The blossom could not then elope

To Persia, where in garden grown,
It might make Allah's pardon known
To mind by lovers' wine unhinged,
To heart by charmer overthrown.

(163) Lullaby

Come the time when I must leave,
Will you sleep on bed of down
When I soft as linden-crown
Cannot whisper? Will you grieve?

When I cannot vigil keep,
When my words, like still song-eyes,
On your limbs, on breasts that rise,
On your lips won't rest or sleep ...

And no more may softly close,
Leave you with your thoughts at ease,
As a garden richly grows
Mute, star-anise filled, with bees ...

(163) Reply: Words for a
Scottish Cradle Tune

Now the quiet night is falling,
You will have a happy sleep.
Softly, how the dark is calling,
May your dream be sweet and deep.

When a gentle rest you've taken,
And the quiet time is done,
In the morning you will waken:
Eyes will gleam to meet the sun.

(164) Pavilion

Even yet through folding doors we feel,
With their glass more green than gloomy rain,
Mirrored an allure that smiles and, clear,
Bright, the gleaming of that gladness dear,
Which, within what cannot lead us near,
Had been hid, transfigured, lost again.

Even yet in stone-frame garlanding,
Bordering the door we touch no longer,
See: a slope toward a secret thing,
And our quiet sympathy made stronger.

Echo-shivers over them will steal
When a wind the stones will overrun;
Coat of arms, as on a letter come,
Far too cheerful, quickly fixed-on seal,

Also talks. How little's thrown away,
All yet knowing, paining, moaning on;
And in leaving by the teary, wan,
Long-abandoned, sad allée,

We must feel how, on the roof-top set,
Urns are cold and cracked and wracked with woes
But resolved to hold together yet
Round the ash of olden Ohs!

(164) Reply: Nikolay Gumilev's "Antiquity"

Within waste wood-bounds of the park
The bittern and the booming frogs
'Mid grassy rustle in the dark
Conduct their evening dialogues.

A house, unpainted, antiquated,
With fog is, somehow, always rife;
The halls, loud-sounding, decorated
With paintings, old, of peasant life.

An atmosphere of ancient ruth:
Where grandpa laid out solitaire;
Each aunt with asked-for, hand-picked youth
In contradances liked to pair.

My homeless heart, how discontented
By this, a dismal legacy!—
Such boring, languid, tired, tormented
Ungolden Age antiquity.

Far better find a craggy slope
Where snow on argent peak may lie,
Where black or ashen clouds dash hope
And avalanches groan and sigh.

(165) The Abduction

Often, a child, from servant-sighs
She's whisked away: the wind, the night
(Within, they seem quite otherwise)
To see outside begin their flight;

But never stormy strength had rent
Apart so hard the giant park
As now her conscience could tormént,
That would her silken ladder get
And bear her far, and farther yet ... :

Till there was nothing but the car.

She smelled it, black, so cold and far;
Around it, stopped, the hunt was still,
And peril stood.
Renounced she found it with the cold,
And the black and the cold remained in her.
In coat-collar crawling, her fear to enfold,
She felt her hair, a comforter,
And, alien, heard a stranger, too:
Iamwithyou.

(165) Reply

Re-dreaming troubled "Alder King"?
The wind is rustling through the leaves;
The youth foresees: the father grieves.

The spirit of the tree by wing
Beswept with envy innocence
And led to ugly underworld
The beauty of perfection, whence
He felt (that bitter Satan!) hurled
By view of what he'd never had:
A father's love for cherished lad.

But here the maiden lives.

I stay with you; fear not a thing,
The riddling song she'll hear,
For One forgives.
It is the Mercy King
That elder is than alder sprite:
From sea, the spirit wind,
That grief has known at night.
She thought that she had sinned,
Yet—a motet will set her right;
The song, with Goethe's twinned,
To dark demurs: in Bach is light.

(166) Pink Hydrangea

The pink, who would accept? Who even knew
That in these umbels gathered such a hue?
As things among the gold their gold may lose,
The red was lessened, as in things folk use.

They little would appear to care for pink.
Will it remain and smile to them in air?
Will tender angels greet it at the brink,
When it is gone, as any fragrance fair?

Or it may be abandoned when it goes,
That it might nothing know when life outflows;
And yet below the pink might green disclose
What it has heard, that fades and wisdom knows.

(166) Reply

So Blake the caterpillar on the leaf
Could hear as it would speak of Mother's grief.
The pathos of our fate we can't but see
In nature, named 'pathetic fallacy.'

Emotion, though, what logic would refute?
In heart's-blood, not in brain, her carmine root.
'Before the flow'rs of friendship faded friend-
ship faded." Echoed, yes!, the theme of End.

A singer I became at sixty-one
And psalm in autumn when the flaming sun
Is emulated by the praying leaves;
A knight is kneeling, braced in brazen greaves.

(167) Coat of Arms

Like a mirror things that far it bore
Silent taking in, so is the shield;
Open once, then closed for evermore
Over shapes the glass might yield

Of the beings that in regions far
Dwell, and of their things, realities
That no more to be contested are
(Left, right, switched; for none agrees),

What had been professed and said and shown.
What had fame, obscurity outgrown:
Spangled helmet, shortened, up above,

Which the casement jewel guards in love
With the cover, as lamenting moan,
Rich and upward-pointing, downward thrown.

(167) Reply

Я лилию добуду голубую.—К. Д. Бальмонт

The hybrid of a mirror and a creed,
With old belief in might and pride invested,
No longer, though, in battle to be tested,
It is at once an icon and a screed.

The statements never hence will be contested,
And only an historian would need
The feelings, faded and antique, to heed
In emblems where a reputation rested.

From image will be wrested what we read
Of goals to which the ardent palmer quested
With pilgrim staff and shoon and tardy speed.

Coeval with the Venerable Bede
Are gentry-claims in heraldry well-nested:
For me, be light blue lily heaven meed.

(168) The Bachelor

Lamp on the varied papers left aside—
And night all round, perfusing, as he felt,
The cupboard wood. He well might, lost, abide
With all his sex, in whom he seemed to melt;
The more he read, the more he had their pride,
And they held his, it couldn't be denied.

The empty chairs were proud with stiffened will
Along the wall; complacency would fill
The heavy furniture and make it doze.
The night is pouring down upon the clock
And running from the golden mill-wheel lock
Precisely painted, time outflows.

He caught it not. He'd feverishly try,
To rend, like shrouds from bodies, times erased
And quickly bring them nigh—
And whispered (what more strangeness would be
    faced?);
One letter-writer, as in brave reply
He praised: you know me most!—
And struck with pleasure on the chair-arm high.
The mirror seemed unlimited inside,
Left out a curtain now, a window wide—:
And, near complete, was standing there: a ghost.

(168) Reply

The bachelor, in reading, would escape
Whatever burdened in the present time:
Emerging in a gratifying shape
Were ancient pals, with sweet desire to rhyme.
Then were they genuine, or merely jape?
Ridiculous, the phantom, or sublime?

Why criticize the youth? In truth, he seemed
Not merely to be one who idly dreamed:
He had not mentally remained at home,
But rather long ago and far away
Had sought a solace nutritive, a stay,
To cross a border, to explore, to roam.

And yet he found what only would applaud,
Embrace him for himself: what need to change?
He'd found the perfect friends.
He was no Prodigal: the journey ends
Not with abandonment, that wretches rends,
All expectation meant to disarrange.
But swelling love is never a corrector:
In later years the lauded proves a gaud.
You'll have to leave your father, Squanderer,
And treasured fellows whom your wants prefer!,
Proclaimed the voice of awe, the spoiling Specter.

(169) The Solitary

No: from out my heart a tow'r will be,
I myself beside its border placed:
Where, with nothing left, once more, for me,
Pain, unsayable, and world are faced.

One thing, also, in the over-great,
Which must dark become, with light then filled:
I one longing final face await
Pushed into the never-to-be-stilled;

Outermost, another stony face,
With its inner weights borne willingly
Which the space that would it fain replace
Forces ever blesseder to be.

(169) Reply

Does he dream his own now stony soul?
Or of his ideal, a mentor saint
Pictured irrefragable and whole
In the skies imaginings will paint?

Is it Christ or God? My heart is faint,
Thinking of the pressure of that role:
Hard, unfissurable, free of taint,
How to breathe? Or how conceive a goal?

Dim, arrived a face within my view
From a film of India, with eyes
Guided far behind the blazing blue
Into stilllness, quieting surmise.

(170) The Reader

Who knows that man who sank his face away
From being to a second sort, more still,
That naught but pages turning as they will
At times can interrupt with mighty sway?

Even his mother couldn't be aware
If it is he that, saturated, reads,
With that, his shadow. We, the watchers there,
How could we know what vanished, till—one heeds

A gaze, constrained: all on itself to raise
That was, down in the book below, held back,
With eyes that do not take: a giving gaze,
And through a full and finished world it ranged,
Like children, still, that playing knew no lack,
Made suddenly aware of what's at hand;
His features don't in former order stand—
Forever are they shifted, maybe changed.

(170) Reply

Our features learn to rearrange? A thought—
An odd Picasso portrait—balks the mind;
Less radical we alteration find
That yet may mean our lives have been rewrought.

If eyes are widened, they expand a shine
Upon the brow, and darken chin or cheeks.
The ear that for a subtler hearing seeks,
Turned upward, amplifies the angled line.

And when a memoried aroma we
Would recreate, each muscle near the nose
Will also tense, and reconfigure those.
We'll breathe more deeply when we do it, too,
And strongly alter our complexion-hue.
A taste may move the mouth and change the gaze;
The lauded flavors of our dawning days
Reshape our being and reframe our view.

(171) Apple Orchard

Borgeby-Gård

Come here to see, with sunset done,
On grassy ground our evening green—
As if we'd long ago begun
To get, and set aside unseen,

What now in feeling, memory,
New hope, and bliss now half-forgot,
With inner dark immixed, inwrought,
We'll strew in thought before us, free,

Among the trees of Dürer; these
The weight of hundred labor-days
In brimming fruits can bear with ease;
They patient served, attempting ways

Whereby what measure would exceed
Is hefted and surrendered so
When man one thing alone will need,
Longeval be and, quiet, grow.

(171) Reply

It may beseem insanity
Far rather than a settled calm;
Let deeper breath however be
At once a fiery wine and balm.

The feet that travel round the sphere
Are fleeter-wing'd than Mercury's;
Our frequent fliers, eye and ear:
The eagle on aiguille agrees.

The hands that wander on the keys
And play a sweet computer psalm
Contain the sinewed mysteries
Of sackbut, trumpet, flute and shawm.

The heart and mind that morphed in me
A sanguine-branching Eden Tree
Have birded, too, with neural cheer
Aborning chant of glory-spear.

(172) Muhammad's Calling

Into his hiding place upon the height
What we know well had swiftly happened. He,
The angel, came—tall, pure, in blazing light.
All protest waved aside, he pressingly

Asked—tired, bewildered merchant (that is all
He was), of travel weary, a delay:
He'd never read before, and now to say
Such words—a *wise* man might the task appall!

The angel, though, commanded, showed—indeed
Again showed what upon that page was writ—
Would not give up but urged, insisted: *Read.*

And so he read—so that the angel bowed—
And was now one who had *recited* it,
Was able, heard, had done it, was allowed.

(172) Reply

Fostered alike by beauty and by fear:
Muhammad's kept again within a cave,
Yet now, with no temptation of the grave;
Rather, a charmed and an idyllic cheer.

Enemies gathered, and they came quite near
But found him not. A spider spread a vast
Web at the entry. An acacia cast
Her patterned shadows. And a rock-dove clear

Signal of non-intrusion gave: the place
A man would have to set his foot to pass
Into the cave she rested on. With grass

And twigs and eggs—she halted hunters' pace.
Like the Night Flight, the tour of planet-spheres,
This grace-rich tale the favored man endears.

(173) The Mountain

Thrice ten times and six, a hundred times,
He had tried to paint it, felt his lack—
Ripped away, once more then driven back
(Thrice ten times and six, a hundred times)

Yet the great volcano failed to seize,
Blessed, tempted ever, counsel-reft,—
While the one in outline clad with ease
Lent no splendor-grasp, no hold or heft:

Thousand times from all the days emerged,
Letting peerless night-times fall away,
Begging each in vain that it might stay;
Every image in a minute splurged,
Form-to-form ascent, the soul to lift,
Wide, impassive, no opinion lending—
So at once he'd know, by light unending,
How to rise, to rise above each rift.

(173) Reply

Failure we transcend as we offense
Countermand by simple disregard.
Centeredness within will mean unmarred
We advance, by split made never tense.

When a man the Buddha had abused
Angrily, he answered, "If a man
Gives a present that is then refused,
Who now owns it? Tell me if you can."

"Easy: 'tis the giver who will own it
Since the other man refused to take it."
"If your anger I refuse, I've shown it
Isn't mine, and so your own you make it.
Anger isn't comforting; it can't
Help you if your heart it should invade.
You, the gift's own best possession made,
Are the only owner of that rant."

(174) The Ball

You round one, who the warmth received from two
Hands in your flight above will give away,
Carefree, as if your own; what cannot stay
In objects may, too unimpeded, too

Unthinglike, yet enough a thing in might,
From all the aggregated things outside,
Sudden but not unseen inside us glide:
It glided into you, 'twixt fall and flight

Yet undecided; should he upward swerve
As if he rose with you to greater height,
If then the toss abducting, loosing, bend,

For players from above, with some reserve,
You suddenly new placing may portend
And structure it as in a plan of dance,

Right then, awaited wish by all that view,
Quick, simply, artlessly, mere Nature you,
To fall into the cup of upraised hands.

(174) Reply

I felt the Buddha in the one who tried
To paint the mountain myriad times and knew
That, sandy mándala, soon lost to view,
Each trying, not to be denied, defied,

Or conquered, should be simply gone beyond.
And here I feel the sphere as tossed by Tao:
The why's revealed in loving of the how,
Yet unattached, not fatuously fond.

What's liked is letting be and letting go:
Awareness we will need which can allow
A river-stream that, sinuous, a way

Will find in quiet making, not to know
Save by a willing turning, as in play,
With sounding as of blood within my ear,

A circling amplified by near-borne room,
Which is what in the seashell we will hear
That first-remembered rounding might illume.

(175) The Child

Long they watch, with no high-handed pow'r,
How he's playing; comes at times the round
Real-existent face from profile-bound,
Clear, entire as a completed hour

Which will rise and then will strike an end.
But the others fail to count the stroke;
Gloomed with effort, life-lethargic folk,
Unaware their burden will extend—

Yes, to him: he bears it, then and still,
When he sits, in little garments, tired,
In their waiting-room immured, immired,
Waiting for his time with all his will.

(175) Reply

The child is waiting for his time to come.
They bear, and he is bearing, too, their burden.
They have abandoned hope in gift or guerdon.
His hopeful, rounded face!—theirs flat and glum.

He sits before the grownups' play on stage;
Impatient for the rising of the curtain.
Of this, the timing never can be certain.
He well may find his waiting takes an age.

The goal is got if eye will speak to hand;
But that will happen only if you travel,
Not merely watch a plot unravel:
The journey is the promised land.

(176) The Dog

An image of a world's made up above,
By gazes validated and renewed.
But sometimes, when he's merely wearied of
The picture, secretly a thing is viewed

That comes right up beside, when he is down
And how he really is, not pushed, not placed;
Then, doubtful, his reality effaced
He'll to that picture give, forget it, frown,

So's to hold back, and inwardly direct,
His face, with nearly an entreaty made,
So near to grasping, as with intellect,
And yet denying: for he then would fade.

(176) Reply

I think that Alexander Pope
Conveyed much wisdom, little hope;
Dog-collar verses, richly graven,
By owners noted, bold or craven:

"I am His Highness' dog at Kew.
Pray tell me, sir, whose dog are you?"
Who does not serve what spirit needs
Will lick a hand though fear it feeds.

Who "works for" shop or industry
Or goods-economy or college
Is of that doggy company,
Exhibiting a kindred knowledge.

(177) Stone Beetle

Aren't they near you—what the spirit sees—
The stars? But then, why won't your vision span
The fact that you carnelian scarabees
Have never comprehended, never can,

Until you will agree to carry, too,
With all your ardent blood, the space that on
The hardened shield must press; more near to you
It never was, more mild, devoted, drawn.

It on these beetles many centuries—
Unused, unmarred—has early lain and late;
The beetles, wing close-folded, doze with ease
Contained beneath its gently rocking weight.

(177) Reply

The burden of responsibility
Has lain on beetles pushing balls of dung.
His duty will the servant never free,
Fidelity by elder bard well sung.

He images the god who will the sun
Each day across the heaven duly draw;
And indeflectibly till task be done
He keeps the path, an ardor viewed in awe.

The laws of Ra must weigh upon his back
Till he the circuit-path at length has run
With holy lauding hymn that feels no lack,
For he the praise of deity has won.

(178) Buddha in Glory

Center of all centers, kernels' core,
Almond self-enclosed and sweetening—
All of this, to all the stars and more,
Fruit-flesh, yours. Be greeted, king.

See, you feel how nothing hangs on you:
In the never-ending is your shell,
There the juice of strength will stand, impel;
From outside a radiance aiding, too,

Only high above, your every sun,
Full, is turned, white-hot command.
Yet in you is only but begun
What must over sunlight stand.

(178) Reply

It is told that but a single thought
Buddha held ten thousand devils could
Swift dispel. No cunning, nothing caught.
Simply something understood.

Deeplier than demon or than god
Breathing under, over and beside—
Molten starry center of the sod—
Seeing, feeling, tranquil-eyed,

Far more free than we from other-will,
You to me embody mother-calm
In the time the mind is lying still
And the mulling winds embalm.

BOOKS OF ORIGINAL AND TRANSLATED VERSE
BY MARTIN BIDNEY

Series: East-West Bridge Builders

Volume I: *East-West Poetry:*
A Western Poet Responds to Islamic Tradition in Sonnets,
Hymns, and Songs
State University of New York Press

Volume II: J. W. von Goethe, *East-West Divan:*
The Poems, with "Notes and Essays": Goethe's
Intercultural Dialogues
(translation from the German with original
verse commentarics)
State University of New York Press

Volume III: *Poems of Wine and Tavern Romance:*
A Dialogue with the Persian Poet Hafiz
(translated from von Hammer's German versions,
with original verse commentaries)
State University of New York Press

Volume IV: *A Unifying Light: Lyrical Responses*
to the Qur'an
Dialogic Poetry Press

Volume V: *The Boundless and the Beating Heart*
Friedrich Rückert's The Wisdom of the Brahman
Books 1–4 in Verse Translation with Comment Poems
Dialogic Poetry Press

Volume VI: *God the All-Imaginer:*
Wisdom of Sufi Master Ibn Arabi in 99 Modern Sonnets
(with new translations of his Three Mystic Odes,
27 full-page calligraphies by Shahid Alam)
Dialogic Poetry Press

Volume VII: *Russia's World Traveler Poet:*
Eight Collections by Nikolay Gumilev:
Romantic Flowers, Pearls, Alien Sky, Quiver, Pyre,
Porcelain Pavilion, Tent, Fire Column
Translated with Foreword by Martin Bidney
Introduction and Illustrations by Marina Zalesski
Dialogic Poetry Press

Volume VIII: *Six Dialogic Poetry Chapbooks:*
Taxi Drivers, Magritte Paintings, Gallic Ballads,
Russian Loves, Kafka Reactions, Inferno Update
Dialogic Poetry Press

Volume IX: *A Lover's Art: The Song of Songs in Musical*
English Meters, plus 180 Original Love Poems in Reply—
A Dialogue with Scripture
Dialogic Poetry Press

Volume X: *A Hundred Villanelles, A Hundred Blogatelles*
Dialogic Poetry Press

Other Poetry Books by Martin Bidney

Rilke's Art of Metric Melody: Form-Faithful Translations
with Dialogic Verse Replies. Volume One:
New Poems I and II
Dialogic Poetry Press

A Hundred Artisanal Tonal Poems with Blogs
on Facing Pages:
Slimmed-down Fourteeners, Four-beat Lines,
and Tight, Sweet Harmonies
Dialogic Poetry Press

Shakespair: Sonnet Replies to the 154 Sonnets of William
Shakespeare
Dialogic Poetry Press

Alexander Pushkin, *Like a Fine Rug of Erivan:*
West-East Poems
(trilingual with audio, co-translated from Russian and
co-edited with Bidney's Introduction)
Mommsen Foundation / Global Scholarly Publications

Saul Tchernikhovsky, *Lyrical Tales and Poems*
of Jewish Life
(translated from the Russian versions of
Vladislav Khodasevich)
Keshet Press

A Poetic Dialogue with Adam Mickiewicz:
The "Crimean Sonnets"
(translated from the Polish, with Sonnet Preface,
Sonnet Replies, and Notes)
Bernstein-Verlag Bonn

Enrico Corsi and Francesca Gambino,
Divine Adventure: The Fantastic Travels of Dante
(English verse rendition of the prose translation
by Maria Vera Properzi-Altschuler)
Idea Publications

Literary Criticism

Patterns of Epiphany: From Wordsworth to Tennyson,
Pater, and Barrett Browning
Southern Illinois University Press

Blake and Goethe: Psychology, Ontology, Imagination
University of Missouri Press

[For e-books on Mickiewicz, Pushkin, and Bjerke
see martinbidney.com]

.

Made in the USA
Coppell, TX
02 December 2021

66957957R00266